survival guide for the End of Days

thirtysix.org

Survival Guide For the End of Days

ISBN 9781520932057

Any questions that arise regarding the above should be dealt with by writing directly to Rabbi Winston at: webmaster@thirtysix.org.

Published by:
Thirtysix.org
355 St. Clair Avenue W.
Toronto, Ontario
Canada   M5P 1N5

I heard in London from the holy Rabbi Elchanan Wasserman, quoting the Chofetz Chaim, that our Rabbis say that the war of Gog and Magog will be threefold. After the First World War, the Chofetz Chaim said that it was the first battle of Gog and Magog, and that in about 25 years time, a second world war would occur that would make the first one seem insignificant. And then, there will be a third battle . . . Rav Elchanan concluded that one must suffer the pangs of Moshiach. However, the wise man will quietly prepare himself during that time, and perhaps he will merit to see the comforting of Zion and Jerusalem. Leiv Eliyahu, Shemos, p.172

ARMAGEDDON. WHATEVER THE originally
meant,[1] it has come to refer to one thing: the End-
of-Days. As to exactly what is predicted to happen
at that time depends upon one's religious outlook,
but at least when it comes to the Jewish take on
this age-old topic, it is based upon warnings from
the prophets:

> "It shall come to pass on that day, on the day
> that Gog shall come against the Land of Is-

---

[1] Actually, the word Armageddon is not Jewish in origin, and is
probably derived from the words, Har Megiddo, or Mountain of
Megiddo, which is in Israel. According to some non-Jewish versions
of the End-of-Days, this is where the final catastrophic battle will
occur to bring history as we know it to an end. However, today, for
many people around the world, it could just as easily refer to a
planet-killing comet.

rael," says the Lord, God, "My fury shall rise up . . . And, in My jealousy, in the fire of My anger, I have spoken—surely on that day there will be a great shaking in the Land of Israel. The fish of the sea and the birds of the sky and the beasts of the field, and all the creeping things that creep upon the earth, and all the people who are upon the face of the earth, shall shake at My Presence; the mountains shall be destroyed, the steep places shall fall, and every wall will fall to the ground." (Yechezkel 38:18-20)

Some people believe in such prophecies whole-heartedly. They have already been preparing for such global disaster for years, if not decades, but usually, they are written off as being mentally-unstable.

It is because of what they do that they are marginalized, acting as if the End-of-Days is already upon us while the vast majority of the world believes that, as bad as things are today, it is not yet Armageddon. As difficult as life may have become, optimism bias says it can still get better before it gets that bad.

It appears with recent world events that the doomsayers are correct. There appears to be a financial Armageddon with threats of the European Union buckling under the pressure of failing economies with other parts of the world not so far behind. Even in the U.S., where the national debt continues to climb and the recession continues to linger, analysts speak of a financial cliff that the American economy is dangerously approaching.

Geopolitically, the situation is no better. Iran has nuclear capability. There is tremendous instability in the Middle-East, especially as the U.N. seems set to give the Palestinians independent status, and will, no doubt, push to make the Green Line the official border between Israel and the Arabs.

Mother Nature has also added to world instability, most recently with the hurricane that hit the eastern coast of the United States and did significant damage. According to meteorologists, more natural destruction may be in store.

Even mainstream Torah leaders, who previously avoided the topic, have changed their minds. They are now warning us about things that I began warning about years ago.

So, what is one to make of all of this? More importantly, how is one supposed to deal with what has occurred, and what may be coming up? That will all depend upon what you believe and your point of view. This book presents one powerful viewpoint: accurate and well-sourced that will assist in guiding you during these tumultuous times.

Most forecasters merely respond to what they see occurring in the world, and project their opinions into the future when providing analysis and advice. This book, however, is based on something far more absolute: the words of those in touch with the bigger picture from a Divine point of view.

In 1999, I predicted that something negative and large would happen in the United States to change the way the Jewish people felt about living in America. At that time in history, even with Y2K looming on the horizon, it was not an easy sell. It was a time of relative peace, stable enough financial markets, and a generally positive outlook on life in much of the Western world. It's hard to get people to believe a thunderstorm is coming when there isn't yet a cloud in the sky.

At that time I wrote a book called Not Just Another Scenario: A Novel For the End of Days, a fictional story based upon Torah sources to help those willing to imagine how the events of current history could easily lead to an End-of-Days situation. The book sold out twice, but more because of the storyline than the message it was created to deliver. The world was still too calm to allow people to project negatively into their futures.

Though the world survived the Millennium Bug just fine in 2000, it had a far more difficult time dealing with the immediate and total destruction of the World Trade Center in 2001 by Arab terrorists. To the absolute horror and shock felt around the world, on September 11, 2001, out of the clear blue sky, two hijacked commercial jets slammed into the World Trade Center. Both towers were brought down within 103 minutes, a seemingly impossible feat from an engineering point of view.

The world turned a very difficult corner. Within hours of the attack, I received phone calls, mostly from the States, from people who had heard my prediction and now wanted to know how I knew, and what to do next. Just as the miracles of the Six Day War in 1967 made Israelis talk about the coming of Moshiach, even secular Jews, the attack on the Twin Towers all of a sudden had people speaking about the War of Gog and Magog, Armageddon, and the End-of-Days.

The truth is, Y2K had prepared many for that. Since there was a lot of hype about the potential damage a major computer shutdown could cause world-wide, and the international chaos that would ensue, even prominent news media began throwing terms around like Armageddon and End-of-Days. By the end of 2000, the hype remained only that, but it did re-introduce such Biblical concepts into the general consciousness once again.

What a coincidence.

They quickly cleaned up the shattered buildings that had once been the symbol of America's financial prowess. They even more quickly passed new laws that gave the President of the United States more power than ever before, and created new government departments to deal with the newly-acknowledged threat of local terrorism. Then, as the sun set on the seventh day of Succos in 5761, ushering in Hoshanah Rabbah[2] that year, the Americans finally invaded Afghanistan in search of the mastermind behind 9/11.

Eleven years and a couple of counter- terrorism wars later, the world is still not the same as it was before the attack, nor can it ever be, for the simple reason that 9/11 set into motion events that closed the door on the peaceful and naive

---

[2] The seventh day of the holiday of Succos is called Hoshanah Rabbah, because we circle the bimah in synagogues six more times than we do the rest of the holiday, with a lulav, which contains hoshanos, or myrtle branches, and esrog in hand. The tradition is to also take a bundle of five hoshanos at the end of the prayer for that day and strike the ground several times, symbolizing the beating away of our sins. This is because Hoshanah Rabbah has an aspect of Yom Kippur to it, since it is the day, we are told, that God judges the entire world. This is why it was significant, in terms of Divine Providence, that the attack actually began as Hoshanah Rabbah began, prompting some Kabbalists to declare that the final stage of the War of Gog and Magog had just begun.

world the preceded it.

America changed.

The world changed.

But isn't history always changing? Haven't there always been events that have caused major shifts in the direction of mankind, from which we have recovered eventually? Why now, more than ever is our current world view irrelevant?

These are important questions. We cannot afford to leave ourselves so vulnerable in the face of all these dramatic developments. There is a sense of despair among our people. In 2005, Gush Katif was given away. Soon after, it fell into the hands of Hamas, the number one enemy of the Jewish people, giving the impression that we are moving away from the Final Redemption, not closer to it. This creates despair.

Seven years later, the nations of the world are more intent than ever on giving the Palestinians a state—at the cost of more Jewish land and security. They have already voted in favor of it in the U.N., and this is resulting in additional despair for Jews who think that the path to redemption is straightforward.

What's next? A major war? Many people think so and it certainly appears that this is the trajectory. It seems that it is no longer a question of if, but only one of when, and of sooner, and not of later.

This book will outline what to expect and how to deal with what is happening, by giving you the knowledge and structure to increase your chances of surviving the End of Days.

one
justlikethat

THE FOLLOWING SCENARIO not yet occurred, but could.

It is the summer. The tension in the Middle-East is high, the highest it has been since the Yom Kippur War, but this time, there is a difference. This time the Arabs have the backing of the United Nations. The modern State of Israel has never been so alone.

Two months earlier, the U.N. voted unanimously to grant the Palestinians statehood. The vote carried and the conditions were set: The Israelis had 30 days to leave all areas within the Green Line, with few exceptions. Ma'alei Adumim was to be abandoned, and its 40,000 inhabitants resettled. Jerusalem was to be divided. The Palestinians had made it clear that they will settle for nothing less.

The world was tired of war in the Middle-East. It wanted solutions. The time for talking was over. The time for action was at hand. The world had bigger problems to confront as economy after economy faltered. Even the U.S. was teetering on the brink of financial collapse and needed to devote its attention and money locally. The simplest solution seemed to be to give the Arabs what they want, and to let the Israelis worry about their security.

The Israelis disagreed. From the start they had made it clear that some parts of the country were not for sale, and they weren't about to change their minds now. Three days of meetings in Jerusalem with the Israeli Prime Minister changed nothing. Envoy after envoy had left with the same answer: Jerusalem was not to be divided, and cities like Ma'alei Adumim were going to stay in Jewish hands.

There was talk of an international force being sent in to enforce the U.N. resolution. The Arabs were demanding it. The Israelis immediately responded by stating that any foreign troops caught entering her borders will be viewed as an invading force and dealt with accordingly.

The world was outraged. It demanded punitive action against the "arrogant Jewish State."

As a result, overnight, the status of Jews around the world changed. Anti-Semitism grew rapidly, and the media did its best to fan its flames. The stories, implications, and condemnations against Israel were coming so fast that it seemed they had been pre-written, just waiting for an opportunity to spew forth.

Many Jewish groups around the world, especially Left-leaning ones, were quick to distance themselves from their Israeli brethren, but their gentile neighbors didn't buy it, claiming at protests and in the media: "A Jew is a Jew is a Jew." It was Europe in the late 1930s all over again, and no one was prepared.

At first there were only threats: graffiti scrawled over Jewish buildings and damage to Jewish property. It wasn't long before Jews started getting beaten up. This didn't occur only in dark alleyways, but in places like downtown New York in broad daylight as well. By the time police came to the rescue of the victim, he could barely walk away on his own.

Local governments called for law and order, but did not do enough to enforce it. They recommended that Jews stay in, or at least travel in groups, and to avoid going to places where they might be vulnerable to attack. Some refused to believe that life in America or Canada or England could become unsafe, and threw caution to the wind, usually paying the price for doing so.

Jewish wealth became a hot topic on the Internet as the U.S. economy continued to struggle, with people losing jobs, and food kitchens opening up. Names were mentioned. Statistics were published. There were public cries to nationalize all Jewish wealth, which people claimed only helped to keep Israel strong and defiant.

Jewish businesses suffered, and many were forced to close. Old contracts were broken and new ones were scarce, if they were made at all. Longstanding relationships soured, and Jewish communities around the world found themselves increasingly more isolated and afraid of mobs. As scary as the situation seemed for Israeli Jews, at least they were amongst their own, and could walk their streets with confidence.

Though they weren't yet certain about their own future, they were extremely grateful for having made aliyah earlier, on their own terms, while it had still been possible, and affordable. Those back in the "old country" who had questioned them back then were now sorry they had not followed.

Then it happened. He was considered by many to be extreme, but he stood up in Congress and called for the deportation of Jews to Israel. He was shouted down, but everyone who knew Jewish history understood that these things always start with the extremists. Given the right time of history and the correct circumstances, they become more "mainstream."

It was impossible to believe, but it was also impossible to ignore.

"For the sake of strengthening the domestic economy" laws were passed that limited how much capital could leave the country. For many Jews, however, who had contemplated shifting their assets to safer shores, it was one more major obstacle to leaving America. They envied their friends and family who had had the foresight to move their assets to Israel during better times.

It is really quite amazing how quickly certainty can turn to doubt, how fast security can become insecurity. It was also terribly frightening to see how what seemed impossible yesterday could become so possible today. As recent as a year ago, places like America, Canada, even as far away as Australia seemed like eternal safe havens for Jews. Today it seemed as if they were headed in the direction of World War II Europe . . .

"It never really changes, does it?" a bitter Jewish businessman said to his neighbor as they hurriedly walked home together from Shul one Shabbos.

"Apparently not," his neighbor said.

"How bad do you think things will get?" the first one asked.

"Worse," was all he said, looking ahead into the distance, looking for anyone who might pose a threat to them.

"How much worse?" he asked.

"I don't know," he answered. "And I'd rather not think about it. Besides," he said, fixing his eyes on a column of smoke in the near distance, "I have enough to worry about with the situation as bad as it is right now."

The first one looked in the direction of his friend's gaze to see what had caught his attention. They both stood transfixed for a moment, knowing the source of this smoke. Another synagogue had been firebombed, and they weren't sure whether to run towards the fire to help those in need, or in the opposite direction to avoid being confronted by another anti-Semitic mob.

Turning to his left, the second man read the big black headlines that screamed out from behind the glass of the newspaper box:

UN Force Invades Israel

They had merely been on their way home from Shul, but now they weren't sure where to go. In fact, they really did not know where history would go next. Never before had they ever felt so much in the wrong place at the wrong time as they did now. Just like that, the American Dream had just become the American Nightmare.

two
abc of history

A PLAUSIBLE SCENARIO? That depends upon what you know and what you believe. If a person thinks that history is open-ended, randomly meandering from day to day, from generation to generation, then anything is possible. Current history may simply get better before it gets any worse, as it has many times before.

That, however, is not the Jewish belief. Jewish tradition teaches that history is neither random[1] nor open-ended, and moves from day to day, and from generation to generation, with purpose. There is a master plan for Creation, responsible

---

[1] The Midrash teaches that when God made Creation, He used the Torah as His blueprint (Bereishis Rabbah 1:1).

for everything that happens throughout history, whether man realizes this or not.[2]

The first thing to understand is that history, as we know it, is only temporary. Though many today think that it will remain like this for billions of years, Torah tradition teaches that this stage of history will only last 6000 years,[3] after which an entirely different period of history will begin called Olam HaBah, or the World-to-Come.

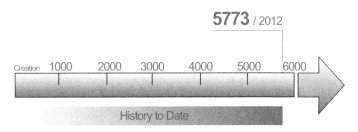

The World-to-Come is eternal and, therefore, the point of Creation; this world is only a stage of human history designed to help us get there.[4] It is the world in which we earn our right to go to the World-to-Come by using our free will to make moral decisions.[5] There is no free will in the World-to-Come, or even as early as the Messianic Era.[6]

However, until that time begins, certain goals

---

[2] The Talmud teaches that, no matter how random events may seem to be, nothing occurs without first being decreed by God (Chullin 7b). The Vilna Gaon explained that the basis of everything that has happened throughout history, or will ever happen, is rooted in the six days of Creation (Biur HaGR"A, Sifra D'Tzniusa, Ch. 5).

[3] Sanhedrin 97a. This is confirmed by Kabbalah (Derech Hashem, Section 1, 3:9; Biur HaGR"A, Sifra D'Tzniusa, Ch. 1), leaving only 227 years left.

[4] As it says: This world is like a corridor before the World-to-Come. Rectify yourself in the corridor in order to be able to enter the Banquet Hall (Pirkei Avos 4:16).

[5] See the book, The Way of God, by Rabbi Chaim Moshe Luzzatto, which is but one source for this fundamental truth.

[6] Succah 52.

are meant to be accomplished, even during this stage of history, as temporary as it may be. One way or another they will occur, and by specific, pre-designated times, which is why certain events have occurred as they have when they have, and why certain events will occur as they will when they will.[7] Divine historic deadlines have a way of influencing the direction of history as they approach.[8]

All of it is for the sake of one thing: the Final Redemption. Mankind has traveled far, always heading in one direction. Mankind gets distracted, but Heaven does not, and even historic deviations drive the world in the direction of the Geulah Shlaimah—the Complete Redemption.[9]

For some, this is simply religious rhetoric; while for others, it is just wishful thinking. For the Torah world, however, it is the inevitable end of a long journey, one that has included all of history ever since man was expelled from the Garden of Eden. It is the inevitable end of world history, the "Point B" at the other end of the line.

What will it look like? What is the endgame?

To begin with, everyone will think differently; intellectual confusion will end. The entire world will recognize the one true God, realize that the Torah came from Him, and strive to live according

---

[7] These pre-designated moments in history are called keitzin in the Talmud (Sanhedrin 97b), or end points. One of the names of the Final Redemption, therefore, is Keitz HaYomin—the End of Days.

[8] There are many examples of this, but one in the Torah is the way Pharaoh had dreams that his regular interpreters could not satisfactorily explain, forcing the release of Yosef from jail, and igniting his meteoric rise to power as per his earlier dreams (Bereishis 41:1-45).

[9] This is alluded to in the second verse of the Torah, which hints to the four exiles the Jewish people were destined to undergo, as well as the Messianic Era (Bereishis Rabbah 2:4).

to it. The world will have one set of values, and they will be based on Torah tradition.[10]

The Jewish people, for their part, will become reconciled with their ultimate destiny, if they hadn't already prior to Moshiach's arrival. No longer will Jews pursue Eisav's[11] world, compromising spiritual priorities for material ones. Rather, they will long to live in Eretz Yisroel—the Land of Israel—and to see the return of the Temple, and the Shechinah—Divine Presence—dwelling within it. They will finally become the light unto nations for which they were redeemed from Egypt.[12]

The gentile nations will take their cue from the Jewish people, who will have reestablished the Sanhedrin to judge all questions of law, be they for the Jewish people or the nations of the world. The nations will have adopted the Noachide Laws[13] as their own. They will even travel to Israel to witness the Jewish people living as a single nation on a single land serving a single God,[14] and support

---

[10] As the prophet foretold: On that day, God will be King over the entire land; He will be One and His Name will be One (Zechariah 14:9).

[11] This is Esau, Jacob's twin brother, and ancestor of much of the world's population today.

[12] It says in Yeshayahu: I am God; I called you for righteousness and I will strengthen your hand; and I formed you, and I made you for a people's covenant, for a light unto nations (Yeshayahu 42:6).

[13] Prior to the giving of Torah, seven commandments were incumbent upon all mankind, six from the time of Adam HaRishon—the First Man—and an additional one from the time of Noach, just after the Flood. They are prohibitions against idolatry, murder, theft, sexual immorality, blasphemy, eating flesh taken from an animal while it is still alive, and a commandment to establishment of courts of law. After the Torah was given (2448/1313 BCE), the Jewish people became obligated in an additional 606 commandments, while the gentile nations remained obligated to observe the original seven commandments.

[14] Rashi, Devarim 33:19.

them. They will see this as their merit. [15]

Miracles will become commonplace,[16] and increasingly more so with each passing day. Even death will become a pleasant experience, as the world moves closer to the next stage of history in preparation for the ultimate stage of history: the World-to-Come.[17]

However, as the Talmud points out, the transition to Yemos HaMoshiach may be a perilous one, depending on how much the Jewish people prepare in advance of it.[18] More than likely, a major war will occur first: the War of Gog and Magog.[19] Should history follow that path to the Messianic Era, it will become more difficult for the Jewish people, and the world in general, before it gets easier.[20]

When history concludes, there can be no loose ends, and the War of Gog and Magog, should

---

[15] The commentators explain that the same way the Egyptians willingly gave of their gold and silver to the Jewish people on their way out of Egypt, much of which was later used to build the Mishkan and its implements, likewise will the gentile world volunteer to help the Jewish people with their service of God in the Messianic Era. See also Succah 55b.

[16] Drushei Olam HaTohu, Chelek 2, Drush 4, Anaf 12, Siman 9.

[17] The Angel of Death will no longer exist, and people will die from Neshikah, or Divine Kiss, a form of death, until this time, reserved only for the righteous people of history (Drushei Olam HaTohu, Chelek 2, Drush 4, Anaf 12, Siman 9).

[18] Rebi Alexandri [further] said: Rebi Yehoshua ben Levi raised the following contradiction, "It says, 'Behold like the clouds of Heaven came one like the son of man' (Daniel 7:13). It is also written, 'Lowly and riding upon a donkey' (Zechariah 9:9). If they merit it, he will come with the clouds of Heaven, but if they do not merit it, he will come upon a donkey." (Sanhedrin 98a)

[19] This was the opinion of the Arizal and the Vilna Gaon, and later, the Chofetz Chaim (Leiv Eliyahu, Shemos, page 172).

[20] After Moshiach comes, a major war will be instigated against the Jewish people, as mentioned in the Holy Zohar . . . Three times in the future Gog and Magog will go to war against the Jewish people and go up against Jerusalem . . . (Drushei Olam HaTohu, Chelek 2, Drush 4, Anaf 12, Siman 10)

it be necessary, will take care of that. It will rid the world of all evil. Only those worthy to enter the Messianic Era shall remain. Who survives and who does not may not be as obvious as it seems to us, as seen from the past. It is one thing to earn reward in the World-to-Come, but not always the same thing to warrant survival in this world.[21]

From the sound of it, the War of Gog and Magog will be World War III. Most likely, many nations will line up against Israel, making it seem as if the destruction of the Jewish State is imminent. The Talmud states that the troubles the Jewish people faced during the previous exiles will pale next to those of the final one,[22] which only means, ultimately, that the salvation in the Final Redemption will be far more miraculous than in all previous redemptions.[23]

How long will the war last? How destructive will it be? How many casualties will it exact? Jewish? Non-Jewish? Will it only use conventional warfare, or will it also be nuclear? What will end it, and how will the world look once it is over?

---

[21] For example, during the Holocaust, righteous people died whereas others who did not keep Torah and mitzvos survived. When it comes to survival in the World-to-Come, righteousness is key, but when it comes to surviving in this world, other factors can come into play, like, for instance, a person's future descendants (Rashi, Shemos 2:12).

[22] Brochos 12b.

[23] The work Ma'aseh Nissim quotes the Ramban as saying that everything that happened in connection with the Exodus from Egypt was a mere sample of what will happen on a far greater scale with the future Redemption (Emes L'Ya'akov).

three

defof history

ALL THAT HAS occurred throughout Jewish history until today is an open book. We know what happened, when, where, and how. It's the future of the Jewish people that we're uncertain about.

It's not that we don't have prophecies about the End-of-Days; we do. However, they are ambiguous at best about what will happen to the Land of Israel, and they say nothing at all about what is going to occur to Diaspora Jewry during the final War of Gog and Magog.

Therefore, perhaps, if someone doesn't mind being a second-class Jew in Yemos HaMoshiach— the Messianic Era —maybe he can safely sit out the transition to this next period of history far from the place of conflict.[1]

When it comes to God and His master plan for Creation, a person can neither run nor hide from his role in it. God has many ways to accomplish His goals, and many messengers to carry out His plans, and as we learn from Yonah the Prophet,[2] it is better, even safer, to embrace that role than to flee from it.

For example, when the Sbarro restaurant, in the center of downtown Jerusalem, was blown up by a Palestinian suicide bomber on August 9, 2001, killing 15 people, seven of whom were children, and injuring 130 others, it underscored the danger of living in Israel at this time of history. However, when Arab terrorists flew two commercial airliners into the Twin Towers in the heart of downtown New York less than 30 days later,

---

[1] Regarding Jews who made aliyah in advance of Moshiach's arrival, the Midrash says: They will become so spiritual that they will be able to fly like eagles, which will astound the redeemed exiles. Upon witnessing this, the Diaspora Jews will become upset, and they will complain to Moshiach, "Are we not Jews like them? Why do they merit to fly and live in an elevated spiritual state, and not us?" Moshiach will answer them, "It is quite well known that God deals measure-for-measure. Hence, those who lived in the Diaspora and made efforts and sacrifices to elevate themselves by moving to the Holy Land now merit purity of soul. They were not concerned about their finances and health, and traveled over vast lands and crossed seas, ignoring the possibilities of drowning, being robbed along the way, or being taken captive by some strange foreign ruler. Being that they emphasized their spirit over materialism and physicality, they merit, measure-for-measure, to be elevated to this lofty spiritual plane. On the other hand, you who also had opportunities to go up to Eretz Yisroel but remained hesitant and reluctant, involved instead with your material status, giving it higher priority than spiritual growth, measure-for- measure, remain physical." (Tuv HaAretz, Praise Of Those Living In Eretz Yisroel When Moshiach Arrives)

[2] Yonah, or Jonah in English, refused to go to Nineveh, as commanded by God, to inspire them to repent. As a result, he was thrown overboard from the ship on which he was fleeing, after which he was swallowed by a large fish before being compelled, by God, to carry out his original mission.

killing close to 3,000 people in less than two hours, it became clear that a Jew can be in danger even 6,000 miles away from the Middle-East.

A person does not die before his or her time.[3] We often use phrases like, "He died early" or "She died before her time," but that is just the way it appears to us. We expect ourselves and other people to live long and healthy lives, but God may have other plans for us, even prior to birth.

What can be affected, however, are the circumstances of one's death. For example, a person may be destined to die exactly at 12:00 am one night, but that can happen either peacefully during sleep, or in a tragic car crash on the way back from a late night meeting.[4] How one dies can be a function of personal merit.

There is a story in the Talmud of Chizkiah HaMelech,[5] a righteous king who almost died 15 years early.[6] His sin? He did not get married in order to avoid having a son that prophecy told him would later turn the Jewish people to idol worship. To save the Jewish people from years of such terrible sinning, he avoided the mitzvah of procreation altogether.

---

[3] The length of one's life is determined by the type of soul he has and from where it comes in the spiritual realm (Sha'ar HaGilgulim, Ch. 35). Also, mazel, loosely translated as destiny, for the most, guides a person's life. We can't completely override mazel, but by learning Torah and performing mitzvos, one can mitigate its impact, though not usually with respect to the day of one's death (Sefer HaKlallim, Hakdamah, Os 13).

[4] In a 100-car pile-up, in which scores of people are killed, not one will have died a second before or after his or her predestined time. God sees to that. However, the same people could have died at the exact same times, except far away from each other, in less conspicuous ways, depending upon the needs of history and the merit of the people involved.

[5] Hizkiah, in English, and He ruled the Kingdom of Judah for 29 years from 3199-3228/562-533 BCE (II Melachim 18:9)

[6] Brochos 10a.

As a result, the prophet Yeshayahu[7] was dispatched by God to inform Chizkiah of his mistake, and its cost. A person's obligation is to perform the mitzvos to the best of his ability, and leave the rest to God. Having failed to do that with respect to this one mitzvah—commandment, Yeshayahu told the king he warranted to die early, and even to lose his portion in the World-to-Come.

Being the righteous Jew that he was, he heeded the prophet's criticism and immediately did teshuvah—repented. However, to try and safeguard against giving birth to an evil son, he married Yeshayahu's daughter[8] and regained his lost 15 years of life, as well as his portion in the World-to-Come.

The question is, though: Had Chizkiah really come that close to losing 15 years of life? Could he have really died before his time?

No, which is why Yeshayahu was sent to him in the first place, to give him the impression that he could die young, so that he would do the necessary teshuvah and continue on with his life. If he had really been meant to die at that time, which would have been his time, then Yeshayahu would not have been sent to him, and the way he died could have atoned for his sin.[9]

---

[7] Isaiah the prophet.

[8] The idea being to limit the chances of a Menashe being born to him and his righteous wife. It didn't work—Menashe turned the country to idol worship for 33 years!—proving once again that no one can second-guess God.

[9] How many times in life do people come close to catastrophe, only to avert it because something "just happened" at the last minute that saved them from the crisis? Or, how many times have people experienced a crisis only find out afterwards that they could have avoided it had they only known something in advance? There is a reason why we find out what we do when we do, or don't when necessary; Divine Providence arranges all of this. Nothing is by chance, because everything is by design: Divine design.

One of the greatest ironies of life is how people can live through dangerous situations, and then die during a time when there is no danger at all. However, it is not really ironic at all if the person walked through the "valley of death" at a time that he was not destined to die, and left it just as "his time" to change worlds had come.

Hence, there is no point in trying to avoid death; it takes its orders from higher up. But, whether a person dies peacefully or violently, sanctifying the Name of God or profaning It, is something that can be influenced by his life choices. A meaningful life results, eventually, in a meaningful death.

Having said all of this, the Torah, and Kabbalah, teach about the meaning and importance of dying in Eretz Yisroel.[10] It is the meaning and importance of living there, especially at the end of history, that is a major point of disagreement today amongst Jews.

This is in spite of the Talmud's advice:

A person should rather live in Eretz Yisroel, even in a city whose majority of inhabitants are gentile, than outside the Land, even if the majority of the city's inhabitants are Jewish. All those who dwell in Eretz Yisroel are like those with a God, and all those who dwell outside the Land are like those without a God.[11]
(Kesuvos 110b)

---

[10] Rashi, Devarim 47:29; Tuv HaAretz, The Advantage of Eretz Yisroel and the Disadvantage of the Diaspora.
[11] Many disregard the importance of this teaching, citing Rabbeinu Chaim mentioned in Tosfos. Rabbeinu Chaim lived during the time of the Crusades, when it truly was life threatening to live in Eretz Yisroel, and extremely hard to uphold the agricultural laws.

The Malbim, perhaps in anticipation of this future confusion, addressed the issue when he wrote:

At the end of their exile, the oppression will be removed from them,[12] and they will be joyous because they will be on the peak of the nations.[13] The gentiles will give them honor and they will be their heads, instead of being disgraced and lowered amongst them as they were at first. Ya'akov will be the masses of the people, and the lesser amongst them; **Yisroel are the great ones.**[14] The joyousness from being at the peak of the nations will be Ya'akov's only, and not Yisroel's, because they will want to return His Presence to Tzion. At that time they will "announce" and publicly proclaim, and "praise" God when they say, "O God, save Your [righteous] people, the remnant of Yisroel," wanting the true salvation of the ingathering of the exiles and the return to Tzion. Then, God will return them: "Behold, I will bring them . . ." (Malbim, Yirmiyahu 31:6-8)

After all, it was our rejection of the Land of Israel at the beginning of our history that has been responsible for all of the exile the Jewish nation has suffered since then. It is only logical to assume that the Final Redemption is just waiting for us to

---

[12] Something that did not really happen until the USSR unexpectedly imploded between 1986 and 1990.

[13] Such widespread acceptance of Jews into the gentile work force is a recent, post-Holocaust phenomenon.

[14] Becoming a Yisroel should be the goal of every Jew, and something for which we are later rewarded. See Drowning in Pshat.

reverse that.[15] Hence, running in the other direction not only does not serve the cause of redemption, it delays it, something for which a person is held accountable.

We learn this from the four-fifths of the enslaved Jewish population that died in Egypt during the ninth plague of darkness.[16] Their crime? They did not want to leave Egypt with Moshe,[17] and consequently,[18] they were made to die meaningless deaths in the Diaspora. It may be a three millennia old message, but it is one that is just as relevant today as it was back then, as the Talmud ominously predicts:

> Rebi Simai said: "It says, 'And I will take you to Me for a people' (Shemos 6:7), and it is also said, 'And I will bring you in [to the land etc.]' (Shemos 6:7). Their exodus from Egypt is compared to their entry into the Land: Just as their entry into the Land [of Israel] was only with two out of 600,000,[19] so too was the exodus from Egypt with only two out of

---

[15] Sha'ar HaGilgulim, Ch. 20, states that the souls of the Jewish people just in advance of Moshiach's arrival will be the reincarnated souls of the Jews of Moshe Rabbeinu's time, assumedly to rectify the sin of the Spies. Hence, before one belittles the value of living in Eretz Yisroel today, he ought to consider what the source of his sentiments might really be.

[16] Only one out of five left Egypt, while four-fifths died during the three days of darkness because they were unworthy of being delivered. (Rashi, Shemos 13:18)

[17] Moses.

[18] Why did He bring darkness upon them? Because there were wicked people amongst the Jewish people of that generation who had no desire to leave Egypt, and these died during the three days of darkness. (Rashi, Shemos 10:22)

[19] That is, of the 600,000 men between the ages of 20 and 60 who left Egypt, the rest having died in the desert because of the sin of the Spies.

600,000."[20] Rava said: "It will be likewise in the Messianic Era, as it says, 'And she shall sing there, as in the days of her youth, and as in the days when she came up out of the land of Egypt' " (Hoshea 2:17). (Sanhedrin 111a)

The following is another detail of history, relevant to this discussion, that is either little known or completely overlooked.

It was towards the end of World War II, just as the tide of the war was finally turning against the Germans in Europe. However, the Nazis had already successfully eliminated much of European Jewry, and the few Jews that were living in Eretz Yisroel at the time lived in dreaded anticipation of much of the same.

The famous "Desert Fox," German General Erwin Rommel, and his Afrika Korps troops were poised to enter Eretz Yisroel from the south (via Egypt), in a coordinated attack with a massive Arab army from the east. Tel Aviv was already being bombed, and the Jewish Agency, in anticipation of the slaughter, had already begun shipping documents out of the country.

In the meantime, Rabbi Yosef Shlomo Kahanaman, seemingly oblivious to what was developing to the south, laid the cornerstone of what was to be the new Ponevezh Yeshivah in B'nei Brak. Shocked onlookers asked him, "Does the rabbi not know of the imminent attack of the Nazis and Arabs? Is it not futile to raise that which will shortly be destroyed?"

However, the venerable rabbi answered his scoffers:

---

[20] The rest having died during the Plague of Darkness.

"The Holy One, Blessed be He, will not allow the enemy to enter His holy land!"

And so it was. Shortly afterward, the situation in Europe forced Hitler to recall Rommel back to Europe, the Afrika Korps were defeated by the British in an eleventh-hour victory in the Battle of El Alamein, and the Arab world was left to savor a victory that never came. As the Axis powers fell, the Ponevezh Yeshivah went up, and it has remained a centerpiece of Torah Jewry to this very day.

How did Rabbi Kahanaman know? Did he simply have faith, and was just fortunate enough to have it rewarded in his lifetime? After all, the enemy has entered and conquered Israel many times before, and has spilled plenty of Jewish blood there over the millennia. What was different this time? To answer this question, we need to look at it from another perspective—God's perspective.

This is the DEF of history: Divine, Eternal, and Full.

four

viewfromabove

THE TORAH RECORDS the following dialogue between God and Moshe, just in advance of the downfall of Egypt:

> God told Moshe, "Come to Pharaoh. I have allowed him to be stubborn, as well as his servants, in order to perform My signs among them, so you can relate it to your son, and your son's son, how I mocked Egypt, and about the signs I performed among them, so you will know that I am God." (Shemos 10:1-2)

These verses say much about God's program for history, specifically Jewish history. And, when it comes to God, you can be sure that it is not about showmanship, but about leaving an indelible impression on generations of Jews, and ultimately, the entire world as well: God is God.

Given the status of God today in many parts of the world, we can understand why. In spite of all the signs that there is a God, and that He is actively involved in history, many either doubt or misconstrue His existence. The role of the Jewish people as a light unto nations was to teach the world about the one true God. Apparently, it is a work in progress.

Kabbalah explains that this is not for God's sake, but for man's sake.[1] The greatest pleasure in life is the revelation of God,[2] something we can't really appreciate until Yemos HaMoshiach and onward, and the greatest merit one can earn in life is to reveal Him in the world, what the Torah calls a Kiddush Hashem—Sanctification of the Name.[3]

The Vilna Gaon explained that the entire point of ingathering the exiles to Eretz Yisroel and the Final Redemption is for the sake of Kiddush Hashem, as the prophet has said:

> Therefore say to the House of Israel: "Thus says the Lord God: 'I do not do this for your sake, O House of Israel, but for My holy Name,

---

[1] Chelek HaBiurim, Drushei Igulim v'Yoshar, Anaf 1, Os 1.

[2] Derech Hashem, Section 1, 2:3; Chelek HaBiurim, Drushei Igulim v'Yoshar, Anaf 1, Os 1.

[3] It happens also to be one of the 613 Mitzvos, and therefore incumbent on every Jew. Basically, any act, speech, or even thought that increases the reality of God within Creation, even if others do not consciously recognize the difference, is considered to sanctify the Name of God. Hence, Kiddush Hashem does not require others to witness the act, although that can increase the intensity of the Kiddush Hashem, and it an occur even if the source of the Kiddush Hashem is ridiculed as a result.

which you have profaned amongst the nations, to which you have gone. And I will sanctify My great Name, which has been profaned amongst the nations, which you have profaned in the midst of them, and the nations shall know that I am the Lord,' says the Lord, God, 'when I shall be sanctified through you before their eyes. For I will take you from amongst the nations, and gather you out of all the countries, and will bring you into your own land.' " (Yechezkel 36:22-24)

In short, the Diaspora is not where a Jew belongs. It may be where he has to go sometimes, but being there is never ideal. A Jew belongs in Eretz Yisroel with the rest of his nation, living on one land and under one king:

> Thus says the Lord, God: "Behold, I will take the Children of Israel from amongst the nations to which they have gone, and I will gather them from every side, and bring them into their own land, and I will make them one nation in the land, upon the mountains of Israel, and one king shall be king to them all." (Yechezkel 37:21-25)

When Jews are unable to live in Eretz Yisroel, it gives the world the impression that God has rejected the Jewish people, or worse, He never chose them. It weakens people's belief in Torah and Divine Providence, which is a Chillul Hashem, or a Profanation of the Name,[4] and it blurs the omnipotence of God in the eyes of the world.

This has been true in general throughout the millennia, but it will certainly be true just in advance of the Final Redemption. After all, what message does it send to one's fellow Jews, to the gentile world, and above all, to God, if a Jew runs in the opposite direction of the redemption as it approaches?

Think about it. If you were God, and the goal was to validate the reality of God in the eyes of the world, and the Divinity of Torah to all those who question it, would you protect the Jews of Eretz Yisroel from their enemies, or allow them to be devoured by them? Would you abandon your children who have made sacrifices to live on your land, and spare the ones who have distanced themselves from it?

And let's not forget that the Presence of the Shechinah—Divine Presence—in Chutz L'Aretz—the Diaspora, the reason for Jewish safety and prosperity in foreign lands, is but a temporary reality; in Eretz Yisroel, it is a permanent one. Hence, once the Shechinah leaves the Diaspora, anti-Semitism, by definition, will return, and with a vengeance, as it always has throughout the last three millennia, just about everywhere the Jewish people have lived on foreign soil.[5]

---

[4] Furthermore, living amongst gentile populations tends to lead to additional Chillul Hashem because of the carelessness of some of the Jews living there. See the Glossary for a more complete definition.

[5] When the Jewish people are sent into exile as a function of Divine Providence, then the Divine Presence accompanies them there to protect them and to allow them to prosper. However, to stay longer in the Diaspora than the Divine Presence is to become vulnerable to anti-Semitism and terrible destruction, as history testifies. This idea is dealt with in detail in Drowning in Pshat.

So, that urge to avoid aliyah? Perhaps even run in the opposite direction of Eretz Yisroel? It is worth considering its source, and how it might be misleading many Jews into being in the wrong place at the wrong time of history.

five
historical considerations

UNUSUAL CIRCUMSTANCES HAVE a way of making us consider options we might previously never have entertained. They can make risk-takers even out of the most conservative of people. There were countless Jews in Europe, at the beginning of World War II, who felt it was too dangerous to leave Europe, but who, once the Holocaust began, regretted that they didn't take that risk.

Once upon a time in the West, decades ago, it was only about making aliyah. A Jew left America, or Canada, or England, to live in Eretz Yisroel because he or she personally liked the idea. They didn't have to run away from anti-Semitism or to protect their personal wealth.

Today, however, the situation is different. Over the past decade, the circumstances have changed and now aliyah has become more of an imperative. The fact that so few Jews in the West agree is no surprise, since historically, and almost without exception, we have overstayed our welcome —and have paid dearly for it.[1]

The following are some historical considerations necessary for coming to terms with our current period of history.

ONE: Current Jewish History

The very fact that Israel, with a population of only around 6,000,000 Jews and surrounded by hundreds of millions of enemies, has survived until today speaks volumes about its special Providence. These enemies have the will and the means to destroy the small Jewish State many times over, and have shown on many occasions how they are not concerned about world opinion.

Yet, Israel has not only survived, it has thrived. Forced to hold a sword in one hand while building the country with the other,[2] the Jewish people have been unusually successful at both. The entire history of the country is counter-intuitive,[3] suggesting that, despite all of its problems

---

[1] It is unlikely to be any different at the end of this last exile as well, as Rashi writes: Great is the day of the ingathering . . . as if God Himself will have to take each person by the hand to return him from his place [in exile] (Rashi, Devarim 30:3).

[2] See Nechemiah 4:9-12.

[3] As Mark Twain once said: "The Jews constitute but one percent of the human race. It suggests a nebulous dim puff of star dust lost in the blaze of the Milky Way. Properly the Jew ought hardly to be heard of, but he is heard of, has always been heard of. He is as prominent on the planet as any other people, and his commercial importance is extravagantly out of proportion to the smallness of his bulk . . ." (Mark Twain, Concerning The Jews, Harper's Monthly, September 1899)

and known drawbacks, there is something authentically Divine about its continued existence.[4]

What if the formation of the Jewish State in 1948 was actually part of the redemption process, as well as everything that has happened since then? That would certainly help to explain so much of what has transpired over the last six decades, both good and bad.

It would also be good reason for Diaspora Jews to re-think their relationship to Eretz Yisroel. The fact that the State was founded by secular Jews and is still governed by non-Torah Jews doesn't change any of that, given our murky past.[5]

TWO: The End of the Line

As mentioned previously, history as we know it transitions into the Messianic Era. What was not previously mentioned is that the Messianic Era transitions into another period of history called Techiyas HaMeisim, or the Resurrection of the Dead, in preparation for entering the World-to-Come.

Mankind has not always been as physical as he is today. Jewish Mysticism explains that once human skin was made of light, only becoming physical as it is now because of his eating from the

---

[4] As King David wrote: This is from God, that which is wondrous in our eyes (Tehillim 118:23).

[5] The fact that the return to the Jewish homeland, after thousands of years in exile, occurred through secular Zionists should not surprise anyone familiar with Jewish history. More often than not, the ancestors of Moshiach have had murky beginnings, and as Kabbalah teaches, our lack of willingness to do what is necessary to bring the redemption compels God to work through backdoor means to move history in the direction of the Final Redemption (Sha'ar HaGilgulim, Ch. 38). See my book, Drowning in Pshat, for a more thorough discussion of this very important topic.

Tree of Knowledge of Good and Evil.[6] In order to enter the World-to-Come, a purely spiritual world, that will have to change; man will have to regain his former level of existence.

This, Tradition teaches, is the reason for resurrection. By dissolving in the ground after death and then being rebuilt anew, every person will come back on a higher spiritual plane better suited for eternal life after Year 6000.[7]

During this period of history there will be no evil, and therefore, no free-will. It will be quite a perfect existence, unlike any mankind has ever experienced since leaving the Garden of Eden. And, astonishingly, it begins on this side of Year 6000, even as early as 13 years from now, 40 years after the beginning of Kibbutz Golios—the Ingathering of the Exiles:

> The period of time from death to resurrection will be the same for everyone, but the day of death for each person will not be the same. As a result, the period of dying and resurrection will last many generations, with righteous people who have already died resurrecting at the beginning of the period, which will begin immediately after the 40 years of Kibbutz Golios—the Ingathering of the Exiles. This is what it says in the Midrash Ne'elam (Parashas Toldos 140a): There will be many resurrections, and the entire time of resurrection, according to Rebi Yehudah, will be from 40 years after Kibbutz Golios, when the

---

[6] Drushei Olam HaTohu, Chelek 2, Drush 4, Anaf 12, Siman 9.

[7] The Mishnah says that one who does not accept this idea as being based in Torah forfeits his portion in Eternity (Sanhedrin, 11:1; 90a).

first resurrections will begin, and continue until the last resurrection, at the end of 210 years. According to Rebi Yitzchak, 214 years . . . However, the rest of the holidays allude only to lights of rectification of Yemos HaMoshiach, after which begins the period of Techiyas HaMeisim [that continues] until the end of the 6000 years. (Drushei Olam HaTohu, Chelek 2, Drush 4, Anaf 12, Siman 9-10)

Doing the math, 214 years in advance of 6000 would be the year 2026. Forty years prior to that would have been 1986, meaning that we would now be 26 years into the period of time called Kibbutz Golios. This would also help to explain a lot of the history of the last two decades.[8]

THREE: Prophecy

Back in 1948, a lot of doubt surrounded the formation of the Jewish State, its direction, and how long it might last. Some 64 years, and 6,000,000 people later, the Jewish State stands strong and in a constant state of growth. Even religious Jews who rejected the validity of the State have been benefactors of its existence and infrastructure.

How many peoples have been completely exiled from their land for thousands of years, only to

---

[8] Such as, for example, the sudden and unexpected collapse of the U.S.S.R. during the late 80s, which resulted in a mass exodus of Russian Jews to Israel, as well as the two airlifts of Ethiopian Jews to Eretz Yisroel. Eventually, an organization devoted to promoting American aliyah, Nefesh b'Nefesh, also came into existence at this time with great success. Even Suddam Hussein's risky incursion into Kuwait in 1990, and the Persian Gulf War that followed, can be explained in terms of this timeline of Kibbutz Golios, as discussed in Drowning in Pshat.

return to it after millennia with miraculous success? How many nations, for whom this has happened, has it been prophesied thousands of years in advance?

> I will remember the land, which will have been left behind by them, enjoying its sabbaths, lying desolate without them. The transgression of despising My judgments and detesting My laws, will [also] have been atoned for. In spite of all of this, even though they live in the land of their enemies, I will not discard them, or detest them to the point of annihilating them, or void My covenant with them, for I am God, your God. For their sake, I will remember the covenant of their ancestors, whom I brought out of the land of Egypt before the eyes of the nations, to be their God. I am God. (Vayikra 26:40-45)

Only one: **the Jewish people.**

FOUR: Anti-Semitism

After having seen what the German people did to the Jewish population of Europe during the Holocaust, we wonder today why the Jews stayed around then. It seems so obvious to us what the Nazis were capable of doing to Jews; why wasn't it as obvious to European Jews of the 1930s?

The same question can be asked about the Spanish Jews of the 1400s, or of countless other Jewish communities around the world over the last 3000 years of a long and often torturous history. It begs the question: Will this later be asked about the Jews of the Western world of our time as well?

The following was taught long ago, is crucial

for a Jew to know, and has been confirmed by history:

> Rabbi Shimon bar Yochai explained: It is a law and well known that Eisav hates Ya'akov. (Rashi, Bereishis 33:4)

In other words, what this means is that anti-Semitism, in advance of Moshiach's arrival, is the norm, and not the other way around. If the Jewish people go anywhere in the world and are treated with respect and allowed to prosper, it is a miracle, a function of direct Divine Providence, not of the civility of the gentile populations amongst whom the Jewish people may find themselves at any given point in history.

This means, therefore, that the moment God decides to let down the guard protecting the Jewish people and allowing them to prosper in foreign cultures, anti-Semitism will rush in like water breaking through a dike.[9] Overnight, civility can become barbarism, and friends can become the worst of enemies. Those aren't scare tactics. That's history talking.

Generations of Jews who either didn't know this rule, forgot it, or downplayed it, have been lulled into a false sense of security and belonging. Even as the situation changed before their very eyes and became increasingly more dangerous, they remained incredulous, certain that others would not do to them what they could not do to others.

How wrong they were. How wrong we have

---

[9] In my book, Drowning in Pshat, the Kabbalistic reason for this is discussed at length.

been. How wrong we will probably be once again.

So, a miraculous history until today suggests direct Divine Providence protecting the Land.

A mystical tradition indicates that the Messianic Era will end in 13 years, and that the ingathering of the exiles (or perhaps the final phase of Part One) has already begun some 26 years ago.

A remarkable and historic return to the Land, prophesied thousands of years ago, has occurred, as promised, at the end of the fourth and final exile.[10]

There is a return and increase in anti-Semitism world-wide.

These are just a few historical facts worthy of some serious consideration when coming to terms with the events of recent history, and what to do about them. This isn't just opinion. It is destiny talking.

---

[10] Bereishis Rabbah 2:4.

six
reward yes,
safety...

THERE IS ONLY one way to earn, keep, and increase one's portion in the World-to-Come, and that is by learning Torah when possible, and doing all the mitzvos a person can. Kabbalah explains that the net result of doing either actually creates the portion in Eternal Life itself.

However, in terms of surviving danger in this world, it is not so obvious. Countless righteous people have suffered terribly at the hands of their enemies, for one of two possible reasons: They weren't as righteous as they seemed, or Torah and mitzvos do not guarantee personal safety in this world.

Even if there are cases in which the first reason was correct, there have been plenty of cases in which the second reason was true as well. Hence, even though the Torah promises safety and security for obedience:

> If you walk in My laws and keep My commandments and do them ... You will eat your bread until satisfied, and reside in your land in security. (Vayikra 26:3, 5)

sometimes historical circumstances arise,[1] ESPECIALLY DURING TIMES OF EXILE, that override the power of Torah and mitzvos to rain down good on a person in this world.

As we have seen, this can be true about Jews living in the Diaspora, or in Eretz Yisroel. Without question, Divine Providence is more prominent in Eretz Yisroel, as the Torah states:

> The land you are about to possess has mountains and deep valleys, and is watered by rain from the sky—a land which God, your God, cares for, God, your God pays attention to continuously the entire year. (Devarim 11:11-12)

However, the Jews of Eretz Yisroel are no strangers to severe anti-Semitism. Over the ages,

---

[1] Unfortunately, there are many examples of this, but one of the best known is that of the Ten Martyrs about whom we read during the Reader's Repetition of the Mussaf on Yom Kippur, and during the Kinos Service on Tisha B'Av. The Leshem explains that sometimes, when Divine decrees have to be implemented, God will even remove the trust in God that righteous people have, and with which they protect their generation, so that they will not interfere in the needs of history. They, of course, will be rewarded for the trust in God they would have had; it is the generation that loses out because of their lack of protection (Drushei Olam HaTohu, Chelek 2, Drush 5, Anaf 4, Siman 5).

they have been conquered, made to suffer, exiled, and slaughtered, and from the words of the prophets, it is not clear how they will fare during the War of Gog and Magog:

> "It shall come to pass on that day, on the day that Gog shall come against the Land of Israel," says the Lord, God, "My fury shall rise up . . . And, in My jealousy, in the fire of My anger, I have spoken—surely on that day there will be a great shaking in the Land of Israel. The fish of the sea and the birds of the sky and the beasts of the field, and all the creeping things that creep upon the earth, and all the people who are upon the face of the earth, shall shake at My Presence; the mountains shall be destroyed, the steep places shall fall, and every wall will fall to the ground." (Yechezkel 38:18-20)

Great miracles are destined to happen at that time,[2] but will they save everyone?

Jews of the Diaspora, in the past, have often not done much better, and in some periods, even worse. The prophets may not have addressed what will happen specifically to the Jews of Chutz L'Aretz at the End-of-Days, but if previous experience is any indication of what can happen, then it is clear in which direction the events can go.

True, Diaspora Jewry has built solid bases of Torah learning and prayer in Chutz L'Aretz over the last century. Undoubtedly, Heaven is impressed with the amount of ongoing Torah programs that can be found in most major cities

---

[2] Brochos 12b.

around the Western world. This alone, to many, seems to be reason enough to warrant Divine mercy as the world transitions to the Messianic Era.[3]

But weren't the yeshivos of Europe impressive in their time as well, and the quality of learning that took place in them even higher than ours today? Wasn't their level of self-sacrifice for Torah greater than ours, especially given the conditions under which they had to live just to survive? And yet . . .

No one really wants to talk about what the Talmud calls Chevlei Moshiach—the Birth Pangs of Moshiach:

> Rebi Shimon ben Pazzi said in the name of Rebi Yehoshua ben Levi in Bar Kappara's name: Anyone who observes [the practice of] three meals on Shabbos is saved from three evils: Chevlei Moshiach, the retribution of Gihenom, and the wars of Gog and Magog. (Shabbos 118a)

Anyone who does usually is considered to be extreme, even though Jewish history itself have a tendency to get quite extreme, and often not in favor of the Jewish people.

There is always the possibility that nothing bad will happen. There is always a chance that God has tucked away a great miracle just for the

---

[3] There is an idea that, in Yemos HaMoshiach, the synagogues and study halls will fly over to Eretz Yisroel from the Diaspora (Megillah 29a). However, does anyone really know exactly what that means, especially since so many of them have already been destroyed? Furthermore, the Talmud says nothing about the fate of the people who prayed or learned inside of them.

End-of-Days about which we have yet to find out. Maybe Heaven will show infinite mercy when the time comes, and allow us to transition to the Messianic Era peacefully, as unworthy as we may be at the time.

However, the prophets didn't indicate that, and the Talmud predicted just the opposite:

> Their exodus from Egypt is compared to their entry into the Land: Just as their entry into the Land [of Israel] was only with two out of 600,000, so too was the exodus from Egypt with only two out of 600,000." Rava said: "It will be likewise in the Messianic Era, as it says, 'And she shall sing there . . . as in the days when she came up out of the land of Egypt' " (Hoshea 2:17). (Sanhedrin 111a)

The fact that we can't see, from where we now stand, how history can evolve in that direction means little. Did any of the 12,000,000 who died in the Plague of Darkness suspect for a moment that they wouldn't survive that plague? Didn't many of the 6,000,000 who perished in the Holocaust think that they would be safer remaining in Europe than fleeing to America?

Given our past, are we prepared to rely upon a miracle for which we have no source, and just wait to see what happens? Are we prepared to throw past experience to the wind, and simply hope for the best?

Not long ago a well-known, relatively conservative financial analyst went on a money show on national television and spoke about an impending financial armageddon.[4] He cited the economies of many European countries that have either failed or are falling, and the weakening of other major economies, such as that of the United States.

How bad will it get, and who will be affected? We've already seen how difficult matters can become, and we don't know yet that it can't get worse. The question for a Jew is: If and when this happens, where does he or she want to be, amongst the nations of the world, or in a Jewish homeland?

That is something to consider when, for example, businesses go bankrupt and are forced to shutdown, resulting in high unemployment. When that happens, it does not take long for hard times to follow, and for poverty to reach up and touch people who previously had known some measure of material success.

This always leads to social unrest, and where there is social unrest, there are usually high levels of anti-Semitism. Furthermore, if Diaspora Jews maintain any measure of their previous wealth, it will only serve to intensify jealousy and hatred, and make life more dangerous for the average Jew. That is how it has worked in the past.

If social unrest becomes unruly, it might result in Martial Law, and the restriction of various civil liberties. Since governments have already seen what social media can do in the hands of activists, it can be assumed that all of these will be regulated as well.

Angry and frustrated people, of which there will be plenty, always need some kind of scape-

---

[4] He's not the only one, as evident from the book, Aftershock, by David Wiedemer, Robert A. Wiedemer, and Cindy S. Spitzer.

goat. In the past, it has been the wealthy, the government, and in many cases, the Jews as well. Once again, Jews may have to learn to walk looking over their shoulders.

The situation in the Middle-East will only complicate matters.

Soon the world will realize what the Jews have long known: Peace in the Middle-East is not possible, at least not before Moshiach. Instead, the nations will try to impose peace on the Middle-East, mostly by forcing Israel to surrender more land to the Palestinians; which Israel won't and can't do, forcing Israel to defy international demands to pull back to the '67 borders.

More than likely, and in one way or another, this will lead to the next, and probably last, war. And, more than likely, this will be the War of Gog and Magog:

> After Moshiach comes, a major war will be instigated against the Jewish people . . . Three times in the future,[5] Gog and Magog will go to war against the Jewish people and go up against Jerusalem. They will assemble and instigate the nations to go up to Jerusalem with them . . . (Drushei Olam Ha-Tohu, Chelek 2, Drush 4, Anaf 12, Siman 10)

It will start with the Jewish people at a great disadvantage, but it will end with the Jewish peo-

---

[5] According to the Chofetz Chaim, the first and second wars of Gog and Magog were World War I and World War II, respectively. The Talmud seems to count the war between the righteous Jewish king, Chizkiah HaMelech, and his small army, and the Assyrian king, Sancheriv, and his massive army, as a war of Gog and Magog, or at least a potential one (Sanhedrin 94a).

ple being miraculously victorious. It is what happens between these two times, however, that is reason for all the concern for the Jews of Eretz Yisroel. People may have to struggle for food, safety, and all kinds of other aspects of daily life we presently enjoy and take for granted.

Not just Israeli Jews. Diaspora Jews should recall how, during World War II, Japanese Americans found themselves in internment camps after the bombing of Pearl Harbor. There are plenty of those scattered throughout the United States, and should Israel be declared an international threat, it is certain to affect Jews all around the world.

What are the odds of anything like this happening?

Does it really make a difference if God runs the world, and it is His master plan than dictates what happens and when? The odds can be a billion to one that something like this will not happen, but when God is the "one," then it is guaranteed to occur, as it says:

> This is from God, that which is wondrous in our eyes. (Tehillim 118:23)

This is true of the good times and the bad ones as well.

History teaches us that circumstances change quickly. People have gone from slavery to freedom, and from freedom to slavery, in very short periods of time. Even natural disasters, or acts of terrorism, as we have recently seen, can turn people's lives upside down in moments. God has many ways at His disposal to accomplish His mandate for Creation, many of which we may never detect until after their impact.

What we do know, however, is what that mandate is, as the Torah teaches:

To you this was shown so that you could know that Hashem is Elokim,[6] and that there is no one else aside from Him. (Devarim 4:35)

Until now, God has been very patient. He has allowed men to share the credit for the miracles of life and for the successes in history. He has remained silent as humankind has used the gift of life against Him. That ends with Yemos HaMoshiach:

God will be King over the entire land, and on that day, God will be One and His Name will be One. (Zechariah 14:9)

Whatever happens en route to the Messianic Era, it will be to this end. The Chevlei Moshiach that we are destined to undergo will be for the sake of opening the minds of people, and specifically of the Jews, whether they live in Eretz Yisroel or in the Diaspora, so that they can learn this concept and integrate it. If everything has to fail just to teach this truth to man, then it will.

The moment we do finally get with this program, history will turn around, and the situation will begin to improve. Miracles will become in-

---

[6] Elokim is the Name of God used to refer to Divine Providence that works through Nature, which can give people the impression that Creation is on auto-pilot. Hashem is the Name used with respect to miracles, or overt Divine Providence, and it is the mission of the Jew to realize that the same God who performs the obvious miracles is the same God Who performs the covert, that is, natural ones as well, and to teach this to the world.

creasingly more overt, and with them, the reality of God. As it does, evil will diminish, and with it, free will.[7] Mankind will have crossed over the intellectual and emotional threshold from our side of history to the Messianic Era. It will be an astounding moment.

Unfortunately, it will not be a smooth transition for everyone. For people who had invested everything in the belief that God does not exist, or that He doesn't care about what we do, the change will be shocking. For those who believed, but who thought the exile would last many more years, the transformation may be a very uncomfortable adjustment.

Therefore, to be ready then is to prepare now. History can be a bit like musical chairs: When the music stops, where do you want to be standing? In a country of co-religionists in which Divine Providence is easily felt, or amongst nations of the world, whose commitment to our well-being is questionable even in the best of circumstances? It is a question that has to be asked and answered now, because if history has taught us anything at all, it is that tomorrow may be too late.

---

[7] Drushei Olam HaTohu, Chelek 2, Drush 5, Anaf 4, Siman 5.

seven
about redemption

THE FIRST REDEMPTION of the Jewish people occurred with much fanfare. There were 10 plagues that decimated the mightiest nation at that time, followed by the splitting of a sea to free the fleeing Jewish people and drown the pursuing Egyptian army. The events were so astonishing that they have never been equaled.

It was fantastic, but was it necessary? If the point of the redemption was to end the slavery of the Jewish people, it could have been done far more subtly. A serious, but far more common, and therefore, less spectacular plague, could have crippled Egypt, even killed Pharaoh, as Moshe Rabbeinu himself told Pharaoh:

"He could have unleashed His power and destroyed you and your people with pestilence . . ." (Shemos 9:15)

Or, God could have simply changed Pharaoh's mind, as He later did to Achashveros of Purim fame. Apparently, Achashveros had not wanted to kill his wife Vashti, but God put it into his mind to do so to make room for Esther, and the redemption destined to occur through her and Mordechai.[1]

Likewise, God could have made Pharaoh decide not to resist His demand to free the Jewish people, allowing them to leave Egypt without any overt miracles. It wouldn't have been the first time in history that the Jewish people were governed by a benevolent gentile ruler.

But that's not what happened. On the contrary, God went out of His way to perform great miracles for the Jewish people on their way out of Egypt, as it says:

God turned the people around by way of the desert and the Reed Sea.[2] (Shemos 13:18)

He turned them from a straight path to a crooked one. (Rashi)

Apparently, the exodus from Egypt was not only about freeing the Jewish people from slavery. It was also meant to be an education for the Jewish people, at that time, and for all of history:

---

[1] Vilna Gaon, Megillas Esther 1:20.

[2] That is, the Red Sea. Reed Sea is the direct translation of the Hebrew words, Yum Suf.

All of it was to show the Jewish people that God deals with them supernaturally and above measure.[3] All of the miracles did not have to be performed; they only served the purpose of showing [the Jewish people] that they are supernatural and above all the normal worldly processes; the entire order of Creation is prepared to change for them. (Drushei Olam HaTohu, Chelek 2, Drush 5, Anaf 4, Siman 6)

History attests to the fact that this works two ways for the Jewish people, positively and negatively. The very fact that the Jewish people are still here, have returned to their Land after 2,000 years of exile, and have thrived on the Land in spite of the destructive powers surrounding them, testifies to the supernatural quality of the Jewish people in a positive way.

However, the fact that anti-Semitism is so relentless indicates that the supernatural aspect of their existence can cause suffering as well. This is what it means when it says:

It is a law: Eisav hates Ya'akov. (Rashi, Bereishis 33:4)

Racism is natural. Anti-Semitism is not. This is why anti-Semitism can arise even when, and sometimes especially because, Jews have completely assimilated into their host cultures. Racism does not usually surprise its victims be-

---

[3] As the Leshem explains, God does not like to punish a nation prematurely. However, God brought the Ten Plagues on Egypt, even though they had not yet completed their fill of evil, because of the suffering of the Jewish people.

cause it exists for obvious reasons. Anti-Semitism, however, usually catches many Jews by surprise, because they could see no natural reason for it to exist.[4]

You could call it tough love, causing some to feel that they'd rather God not love them so much, or even at all. Once history comes to its conclusion, however, and we finally see what all of it led to, and can then understand the responsibility we had to the master plan of Creation, we will appreciate the way God cared for His people and every aspect of that care.

What will really make this love clear is the Final Redemption, especially after the long and often torturous history the Jewish people will have endured until that time. If ever God proves His love for His people, it will be then, and after all we will have gone through, the final act of history promises to be incredibly miraculous and dramatic, in the positive sense.

You will want to be a part of it, anyway you can. You will want to be included, in whatever capacity possible. That may be hard to appreciate at this stage of history while still so integrated in Western society as we are used to it, but that will change: sooner than later.

Making aliyah in advance is like buying front row seats for the final act of history. If that is where all of the action is going to be, then that is where all the most important and spectacular miracles are going to occur. A major part of God showing His love for His people is in showing His

---

[4] Hitler should never have risen to power, should never have been able to take over Germany, should never have been able to go to war, and should never have been able to carry out the Holocaust. He did. It was a miracle, but not the kind we want.

love for their Land as well:

> The Holy One, Blessed is He, said to Moshe: "Eretz Yisroel is dear to Me, as it says, 'a land which God, your God, cares for, God, your God pays attention to continuously the entire year' (Devarim 11:12), and the Jewish people are dear to Me, as it says, 'For God has loved you' (Devarim 7:8)." The Holy One, Blessed is He, said, "I will bring the Jewish people, who are dear to Me, to Eretz Yisroel, which is dear to Me." (Yalkut Reuveini, Aikev 110)

A redemption is only as great as the problems that it solves. If the Jews of Moshe Rabbeinu's time had only suffered mild anti-Semitism, would they have made such a big deal about leaving Egypt? Not really. The generation that went out would have been grateful, but the next one born into freedom would have forgotten completely about their parents' hardships.

Hence when it comes to Jewish redemptions, it is always darkest before the dawn. God makes sure of that, so that the redemption He brings is worth celebrating and remembering, so that we, the Jewish people, can always recall His great love for us. That is a fundamental of Jewish history.

This is why, when Jewish history becomes darkest, it is time to prepare for great miracles and a spectacular redemption. This is what Mordechai meant when he told Esther:

> "Do not imagine that you will be able to escape in the king's palace any more than the rest of the Jews. For if you continue to remain silent

at a time like this, relief and salvation will come to the Jews from another place, while you and your father's house will perish. And, who knows whether it was for such a time as this that you attained the royal position!" (Esther 4:13)

A Jew needs to know and understand this about Jewish history, in order to avoid being frightened away from Eretz Yisroel at a time when we should be running there. Without such knowledge, he can't look past the current negative reality into the upcoming positive one, in order to be a part of the Final Redemption.

However, is it all or nothing? If someone is just not going to make aliyah in advance of the redemption, is there anything else he or she can do to be a part of it?

The guiding principle is this:

You will arise and show mercy to Tzion, for the time to favor her, the appointed time will have come. For, Your servants have wanted her stones and have cherished her dust. (Tehillim 102:14-15)[5]

The author, Dovid HaMelech—King David, a prophet, it is talking about the time of the Final Redemption, the "appointed time." According to what he has written, the key to Divine mercy at that time will be a love of Eretz Yisroel; we'll have to "want her stones" and "cherish her dust."

For many, this is somewhat counter-intuitive.

---

[5] See Kesuvos 112a for examples of rabbis who, based upon this verse, went to great lengths to live in Eretz Yisroel.

Indeed, it is nothing short of amazing how Eretz Yisroel has come to matter so little to so many Jews today when that is the reason the Jewish nation was first exiled back in the time of the Spies.

Furthermore, the Talmud states:

> Three wonderful gifts were given by The Holy One, Blessed is He, to the Jewish people, and all of them were given through hardship. They are: Torah, Eretz Yisroel, and the World-to-Come. (Brochos 5a)

Like the Jews of Moshe Rabbeinu's time, many today assume that loyalty to God and Torah is Eretz Yisroel enough. But, if the Generation of the Spies paid so dearly for their error,[6] what will happen to those in this generation who perpetuate it?

> The exodus from Egypt liberated only one out of five Jews—and some say one out of every 50—because all those who were bound to Egypt and did not want to depart died in the three days of darkness and were not privileged to leave. That is, only those who desired redemption with all their hearts were redeemed. The Final Redemption, likewise, depends upon our yearning. (Ohr Yechezkel, Emunas HaGeulah, p. 288)

---

[6] According to Rebi Akiva, the Generation of the Spies forfeited their lives in this world, and their portions in the World-to-Come (Sanhedrin 10:3).

Therefore, what follows are some suggestions for those for whom making aliyah may be too big a jump at this time. These are some steps in the right historical direction.

ONE: Investment

Open an Israeli bank account, for starters (if you haven't already), and continuously make deposits. Once the money arrives at your Israeli bank, convert into shekels. This shows that you don't only face east when praying, but also when building towards the future.

Better yet, if you can afford to, buy a piece of Eretz Yisroel, either by yourself or in partnership with others. It can simply be an empty lot, or it can be an existing apartment, which you can rent out in the meantime. The time is coming when investing in foreign countries will become either against the law or extremely restricted. Now is the time, if it is not already too late.

The Talmud points out that Lot prospered in Sodom while he lived there, but when God finally decided to lower the boom on the place, he barely left with his own life.[7] All the property Lot had accumulated there was left behind and destroyed, not unlike what has happened to Jewish property at the end of almost every exile.

We do not yet know what will happen to the nations of the world, or when, especially as they become increasingly more liberal, and undermine some of the most important fundamentals of Creation. Move capital to Eretz Yisroel now, while you can, and while it counts.

---

[7] Yerushalmi, Sanhedrin 54b.

TWO: Live Through Others

The Vilna Gaon, when explaining in his time why the Jews of Eretz Yisroel are dependent upon financial support from Jews in the Diaspora, gave an answer that is, at first, also counter-intuitive. He explained that it is for the benefit of Diaspora Jews, and not just the Jews of Israel.[8]

This is because Jewish history is about redemption, and only redemption. When we have it, we must work to keep it; when we are in exile, we must work to regain it. It can take decades, centuries, or even millennia, but everything we do as a people in exile is for the sake of bringing about the Final Redemption.

That is a lot easier to see and experience when a Jew lives in Eretz Yisroel. Everything he does, by definition, contributes to redemption, especially when he builds the country with his own two hands, something that Diaspora Jews can only appreciate from the distance.

However, to allow Jews outside of Eretz Yisroel to have a portion in the Final Redemption, explained the Vilna Gaon, God allowed them to participate in its building through their money. He made the Jews of Eretz Yisroel financially needy to give Diaspora Jews a chance to be part of the redemption through the people in Eretz Yisroel that they help, or the contributions they make to the infrastructure of the country, especially to places that are central to the redemption process.

---

[8] It is a decree and an act of mercy that the settlement of Eretz Yisroel will be built through tzedakah. For, The Holy One, Blessed is He, wanted to give all Jews, near and far, the merit of having a portion in the building of the inheritance of God, as it says, "They gathered money from all of the Jewish people to fortify the House of God" (Divrei HaYomim 2:24:5). (Kol HaTor, Ch.1:19)

Just as the tribe of Zevulun benefitted from the Torah learning of the tribe of Yissachar, by taking caring of their material needs,[9] a Diaspora Jew can "live" in Israel vicariously, to a limited degree, by financially assisting Jews who live there. It is obviously not nearly as meaningful as actually living on the Land itself—

> The Holy One, Blessed is He, said, "I will bring the Jewish people, who are dear to Me, to Eretz Yisroel, which is dear to Me." (Yalkut Reuveini, Aikev 110)

—but it is also far better than doing nothing at all to get there.

THREE: Eretz Yisroel Consciousness

Eretz Yisroel is not only a geographical location, it is also a frame of mind. Unfortunately, many think that this means that wherever they are learning Torah and performing mitzvos in the world, they have the status, somewhat, of living in Eretz Yisroel. There is truth to that, but not necessarily to the extent that people want to believe.

As mentioned earlier, the Talmud states:

> Three wonderful gifts were given by The Holy One, Blessed is He, to the Jewish people, and all of them were given through hardship. They are: Torah, Eretz Yisroel, and the World-to-Come. (Brochos 5a)

There is no better way to show one's appreciation for a gift than to use it the way it was meant

---

[9] Devarim 33:18; Rashi, Bereishis 49:13.

to be used by the giver. Facsimiles just don't cut it, unless it is impossible to use the real thing and using the facsimile clearly indicates a longing for the real gift.

There are no physical substitutes for Eretz Yisroel, and there are certainly no spiritual ones as well. Nevertheless, there is a way to take Eretz Yisroel into the Diaspora with us, something we have done for thousands of years and on countless occasions, something that we learned from our Forefather Ya'akov Avinu.[10] It is called, Kabbalistically, Shechinah b'Golus,[11] or, the Divine Presence in Exile.

I should preface this by saying that this idea only works on condition, that condition being that a Jew is in the Diaspora for the right reasons, reasons with which God would agree.[12] After all, we can't expect God to look out for us in foreign lands if we're in them for the wrong reasons, can we?

For example, Ya'akov Avinu left Eretz Yisroel unwillingly. He was compelled to go into the Diaspora to save his life since Eisav was intent on murdering him. Additionally, he left to fulfill the wishes of his parents, who sent him out to find a wife. These were the wild horses necessary to drag Ya'akov Avinu out of his beloved land.

But, even with the right reasons to leave Eretz Yisroel, he still hesitated to go until after he made the following declaration:

> Then Ya'akov took a vow saying, "If God will be with me, and He will guard me on this way

---

[10] Jacob, Our Father.
[11] The Divine Presence in Exile.
[12] Some of these reasons are listed in the last mishnah of Kesuvos.

that I am going; and He will give me my bread to eat and clothes to wear; and I will return in peace to my father's house, and God will be God to me—then this stone which I have set up as a pillar shall become a house of God, and whatever You will give me, I shall surely tithe it to You." (Bereishis 28:20-22)

If we analyze what is unique about Eretz Yisroel, at least as far as we can see, it is the level of Divine Providence one enjoys while living there. It is the land of Hashgochah Pratis—Personal Providence—as opposed to Hashgochah Klallis—General Providence, the level of the nations of the world. Hence the Torah states:

I am God your God Who took you out of the land of Egypt, to give you the land of Canaan, to be your God. (Vayikra 25:38)

On the level of Hashgochah Pratis, it is far easier to maintain a God-consciousness than it is on the level of Hashgochah Klallis. This is why, after being forced into exile, Dovid HaMelech said the following about himself:

"For they have driven me out this day that I should not cleave to the inheritance of God, saying: 'Go, serve other gods'." (I Shmuel 26:19)

and the Talmud concludes:

Did someone tell Dovid, "Serve other gods"? Rather, [this is intended] to tell you that whoever lives outside the Land may be regarded as one who worships idols. (Kesuvos 110b)

Therefore, it follows, if there was a way to bring at least some of the level of Divine Providence of Eretz Yisroel into the Diaspora with the Jewish people, then the borders of Eretz Yisroel could be extended somewhat, at least spiritually, to incorporate them while physically living outside of the Land. This is called Shechinah b'Golus, what Ya'akov Avinu did with his vow, and it is the reason for the protection and success the Jewish people have enjoyed in foreign lands, when they have had it.

But remember: it only works if a Jew is in Chutz L'Aretz for the right halachic and hashkofic reasons, something which is not always as obvious as people think. In fact, one of the best litmus tests of this is the level of love and yearning one has for Eretz Yisroel, and for living there. For, anyone who remains in the Diaspora, when they'd much rather be in the Holy Land, must have a good reason to be in Chutz L'Aretz.

Lest people delude themselves, they should recall that many from the Torah world who perished in the Holocaust thought that they would be safer, physically and spiritually, in Europe than anywhere else. In the end, as history makes clear, they were wrong about both. They may have died sanctifying the Name of God, but they died nonetheless, and some even abandoned their faith along the way.

To avoid making a similar and costly error, a Diaspora Jew should first develop an incredible love for the Land and desire to live there. He should read whatever he must to achieve this, and do whatever he can to become real with it. A person should not be afraid to develop a desire for aliyah.

That achieved, it will be far easier to determine if a person's reasons for remaining in the Diaspora are authentic, or if they are just excuses to avoid issues that God would rather a Jew confront.

eight
a matter of trust

RELATIONSHIPS ARE A fundamental part of life, and trust is a fundamental part of any relationship. People are only as close as their trust for one another, and that goes for family, spouses, and business partners. It also goes for the relationship between man and God.

It is one's level of loyalty to others that determines a person's trustworthiness. The more a person is there for someone else, the more a person is prepared to sacrifice for the well-being of another, the more trustworthy that person will appear in the eyes of others. Loyalty is everything when it comes to building and maintaining lasting relationships.

When it comes to God, what do we expect

from Him? What does God have to do to prove His loyalty to us, so that we feel we can trust Him? That's easy: He has to give us what we want when we want it, and make our life as pain free and as joy filled as possible. That's all.

The bigger question is, what do we have to do to prove our loyalty to God, so that He'll help us out whenever we need Him? After all, He can certainly do without us, but we have a very hard time doing without Him. People who think they can just don't realize He's helping them out in spite of their lack of acknowledgement and appreciation.

These are serious questions, concerning which there is the following joke.

Once a man, a sworn atheist, was walking in the jungle when he accidentally tripped and fell off a cliff. Luckily for him, there was a branch sticking out of the side of the cliff, which he just happened to grab onto on the way down.

Hanging from the branch he surveyed his situation, which he deemed to be hopeless, since there was no way to climb back up or down. Finally, in desperation, he began to yell for help, which he suspected was for naught since he had been traveling alone.

"Help! Help!" he called out over and over again. "Is there anyone up there who can help me?"

Finally, his frantic call was answered. "Yes, I am here."

The man, unsure of who it was that just happened to be within earshot of his pleas for help, looked upwards in the direction of the voice, but could see no one.

"You are?" he called back. "Who are you . . . and can you help me? I can't hold on for very much longer . . ."

"This is God," the Voice from above said, "and yes, I can help you."

Skeptical, but in dire need of help, the man called back, "God! Really! That's amazing! Until now I had my doubts . . . but what a time to be proven wrong!"

He thought for a moment, and then finally asked, "Tell me, God, what do I have to do for You to save me?"

"Let go of the branch," the Voice from Above said.

The man thought some more, looked down at what was below him, and up again at what was above him, before calling out, "Is there anyone else up there who can help me?!"

As the expression goes, "There are no atheists in a foxhole," but that is only in terms of calling out to God in a time of need. Desperation can make a believer out of even the most staunch atheist, but only up until he has to take a risk based upon his belief in God, at which point the situation usually becomes, "Once an atheist, always an atheist."

The scary part is that many of us have a little bit of atheist in us as well, even us believers. We may believe in God, that He made Creation, that He gave the Torah to the Jewish people over three millennia ago, and even that He will redeem the Jewish people once again in the future. We may even believe that He runs history, and that everything that happens in our lives is a function of Divine Providence.

We'll talk about all the miracles that God has done for us, the Jewish people, in the past. We'll point out the "amazing Hashgochah Pratis" that resulted, in the past, in some kind of personal or national salvation that clearly showed His hand in the everyday affairs of man. And, we'll thank Him for all of it, in private and publicly.

What many won't do, though, is trust in God for the future. It's not that they think that He can't come through, only that He won't, for some reason or another, and we will have unnecessarily put ourselves at risk. As a result, people would rather stay where they feel less exposed to danger, and limit the need to turn to God to help them out.

This is not a new phenomenon. In fact, it is what brought down the generation of Jews that left Egypt with Moshe Rabbeinu. They too knew that God was capable of doing anything; they had witnessed this first hand. Their only question was: Would He keep doing it for them as they traveled through the valley of death that was the Sinai Desert?[1]

It was a legitimate question, or so they had thought. After all, who were they for whom God should keep changing the world for them? What had they ever done to warrant such Divine intervention? They weren't even sure why God had already stepped in on their behalf so many times before then, which made it that much more difficult for them to believe that He would keep doing it in the future.

Hence, it says about that generation:

Because you did not believe in God and did not trust in His salvation. (Tehillim 78:22)

Nevertheless, they sinned further and had no

---

[1] Drushei Olam HaTohu, Chelek 2, Drush 5, Anaf 4, Siman 5.

faith in His wonders. (Tehillim 78:32)

All because they didn't believe in their own wor-
thiness, which they thought was necessary for
God to keep performing amazing miracles for
them.

The truth is they were only partially wrong.
True, they had been unworthy of special and
miraculous Divine Providence, but:

> Nothing stands in the way of bitachon—trust
> in God—as it says in the Midrash: "One who
> trusts in God will be surrounded by kind-
> ness" (Tehillim 32:10); even an evil person
> who trusts in God will be surrounded by
> kindness (Midrash Tehillim 32:10). It further
> says . . . The Ramban says something similar:
> This is why it says, "Trust in God and do
> good" (Tehillim 37:3), and not, "Do good and
> trust in God." (Drushei Olam HaTohu, Chelek
> 2, Drush 5, Anaf 4, Siman 5)

Do good, in this sense, means do teshuvah for
past sins. After all, the thinking goes, if you want
God to miraculously help you out of a difficult situation, don't you have to first be worthy? No, the
Ramban continues:

> Rather, trust in God does not depend upon
> good deeds at all, but rather, one should trust
> in God whether he is righteous or evil.
> (Drushei Olam HaTohu, Chelek 2, Drush 5,
> Anaf 4, Siman 5)

This is a very novel idea, even for many with
an extensive Torah background. This is especially

so after the Torah, first in Parashas Bechukosai[2] and later in Parashas Ki Savo,[3] indicates that God helps those who learn Torah and perform mitzvos, and punishes those who do not.

This is true. However, what the Torah does not speak out, but commentators do, is that there is one particular trait called Bitachon that can mitigate a person's crisis. It is so powerful and important a trait unto itself that it can work even for an evil person—so how much more so for someone who is at least trying to be good—allowing him to succeed miraculously in spite of his spiritual unworthiness.

Unlike what many people think, bitachon is not simply some background trait. It is not just something you really ought to have if you're going to be religious anyhow, but that if you don't, you can be content with Torah learning and mitzvah performance alone.

It turns out, however, that trust in God is so central to the purpose of Creation that, even when you do not learn the Torah you ought to, or fail to observe the mitzvos you should have, it can still save your day. But, the Ramban added:

> [The verse] concludes, however, with "do good" because if you do not [do teshuvah for past sins], then [Heaven] will exact payment from you nevertheless. The Holy One, Blessed is He, is very patient, and will find the right time to take payment from you (Sefer Emunah v'Bitachon, Ch. 1). (Drushei Olam HaTohu, Chelek 2, Drush 5, Anaf 4, Siman 5)

---

[2] Vayikra, or Leviticus, Ch. 26.
[3] Devarim, or Deuteronomy, Ch. 28.

This means that if someone is in a potentially dangerous situation from which only a miracle can save him, if he sincerely trusts that God will save him, even if he doesn't merit it, he may receive the miracle he needs. Nevertheless, he can get hit by an oncoming truck while happily walking away from his miraculous salvation if he fails to make amends for his past sins after he gets his miracle.

Bitachon saves the day, but it does not wipe a person's slate clean of past sins.

If Bitachon matters so much to God, shouldn't it matter a lot to us? Shouldn't it matter enough to us that we take every opportunity we can to express our bitachon and live in a way that reflects such bitachon?

Learning Torah and performing mitzvos in an environment that does not require much bitachon does little for one's relationship with God, as the Spies in Moshe Rabbeinu's generation found out. They had wanted to remain in the desert, with all the miracles they had enjoyed until then, in order to learn Torah unhampered.

Religious Jews may differ about the meaning of living in Eretz Yisroel today, but everyone agrees on at least one point: you need bitachon to survive there. In fact, we could go so far as to call Eretz Yisroel the Land of Bitachon, because that is exactly what it is, a land that promotes trust in God on a momentary basis. No wonder the Talmud concludes:

> There types of people are destined for the World-to-Come. Someone who lives in Eretz Yisroel . . . (Pesachim 113a)

It is a land that inspires bitachon because it is a land that survives because of bitachon. It exists in a virtual lion's den, and lacks some of the most basic natural resources that other countries depend upon for development. Therefore, it is a land that greatly enhances one's relationship with God in ways that cannot be achieved while living in the Diaspora.

Nevertheless, bitachon only addresses one half of the issue. Though bitachon can save a person from danger, the Ramban made it clear that it can't save a person from Divine punishment if teshuvah is necessary but not forthcoming. The Spies could have easily argued, as we can today:

> Bitachon may allow us to miraculously take the Land, but won't our sins eventually cause us to lose it?

as, in fact, they have more than once in the past?

Yes, and no, and though the yes does not require much explanation, the no certainly does because it reveals another misconception about Divine Providence and the Jew. Indeed, it reveals a whole different dimension of Eretz Yisroel concerning which most Diaspora Jews, and even many Jews living in the Land, have little or no knowledge. It's another game changer.

Reward and punishment, for our generation, is somewhat theoretical. A fundamental of Jewish belief, we know it once existed, we know it is coming up in the World-to-Come, but we have difficulty believing in it on a practical level at this stage of history. We just don't really get to see it in action the way previous generations did, since it seems to happen beyond human sight.

This is not to say that it isn't at work every-day. It means that, at this stage of history, we are not privy to how God operates in the world when He carries out His judgment of people. This is a major aspect of what the Torah calls Hester Pan-im, or the hiding of God's Face:

> And I will surely hide My face in that day for all the evil which they shall have done, when they turned to other gods. (Devarim 31:18)

This is why Yom Kippur is as relevant today as it ever was, because teshuvah and atonement are as relevant today as they ever were. The fact that we can't appreciate how this is true does not change that reality. In fact, to a Jew today, it should emphasize the importance of living in Eretz Yisroel, or at least yearning to:

> Those who dwell in Eretz Yisroel do so free of sin . . . This is the meaning of the verse, "You have forgiven the iniquity of Your people; You have covered up their entire sin, Se-lah!" (Tehillim 85:3) . . . In other words, God has made a "covering" for their intentional sins from their errors, turning all their sins into errors![4] (Tuv HaAretz, The Advantage of Living in Eretz Yisroel)

Unlike the Diaspora, the Land of Israel has a very special spiritual property that makes it Yom Kippur everyday for those who live there, for un-witting errors, accidental errors, and even for out-right sins. It's as if the Land absorbs the sins of the

---

[4] That is, accidental sins, for which the Land atones automatically.

people living there, atoning for them 365 days of the year, 24 hours a day.

> This is how a person dwelling in Eretz Yisroel is free from sin; for performing the mitzvos that are specific to the land, they are granted forgiveness. (Tuv HaAretz, The Advantage of Living in Eretz Yisroel)

One of the reasons why Eretz Yisroel is so special is because there are mitzvos that are unique to those people living on the Land, such as taking tithes on produce and observing the Shmittah—Sabbatical—year. Somehow, by observing these special mitzvos, the Land is able to absorb the sins of its inhabitants, and to later rid itself of the spiritual burden.

> This is the essence of what Rav Elazar meant when he said: "All those who reside in Eretz Yisroel live without sin." That is, if they abide by the laws dependent on the Land . . . When living in Eretz Yisroel and performing the mitzvos dependent upon the land, their iniquities become purified automatically, and therefore do not require the same cleansing and purging processes necessary for those who live outside the land. (Tuv HaAretz, The Advantage of Living in Eretz Yisroel)

This is a remarkable concept, quite different from what people think. The only question is, how far does it go? This far:

The Ramak,[5] z"l, also wrote: "You should know that anyone who lives in Eretz Yisroel is called righteous, even if he does not appear to be righteous. If he was not righteous, the land would spit him out, as it says, 'The land will spit out its inhabitants' (Vayikra 18:25). Hence, since the land has not spit him out, he is certainly called righteous, even if he is assumed to be evil, as it says, 'This is the gate of God; righteous people come through it' (Tehillim 118:20). This means that Eretz Yisroel is called the 'Gate of Heaven,' as Ya'akov Avinu said, 'This is none other than the house of God, and this is the gate of Heaven!' " (Bereishis 28:17). (Tuv HaAretz; The Advantage of Living in Eretz Yisroel)

As mentioned before, the only real way to earn reward in the World-to-Come is through the learning of Torah and the performance of mitzvos to the best of one's personal ability. Furthermore, the Torah tells us that our blessing can increase in this world as well when we do, and can decrease when we don't.

Jewish life, however, is not so simple. Bitachon can be a mitigating factor even when a person does not live up to his or her spiritual potential. And, it turns out, that just living in Eretz Yisroel and keeping the mitzvos dependent upon the Land is also a tremendous merit to have in one's corner.

These novel ideas may not mean so much to some of us now, while God still runs history from under a cloak, but they will one day: History will

---

[5] Rabbi Moshe Cordovero (1522-1570 CE).

sensitize us to their importance. As the Talmud says:

Who is a wise man? One who can see what is being born. (Tamid 32a)

We can see where things are going. Being wise means responding today so that we can be prepared tomorrow for what may come our way. Without question, Bitachon will figure heavily in that preparation, as will Eretz Yisroel, and sooner, rather than later.

nine
ingoodfaith

USUALLY, THE WORDS emunah—faith—and bitachon— trust are used interchangeably, both implying reliance on someone or something without certain knowledge that either will come through. However, it is more accurate and insightful to say that they are interdependent, as the words themselves imply.

The Hebrew word for someone who is an expert at his trade is uman, spelled Aleph-Vav-Mem-Nun, which is very similar to the word emunah, spelled Aleph-Mem-Vav-Nun-Heh. This is because an uman is someone who has proven himself at his expertise through past performance, making himself reliable to others in the future.

For example, you wouldn't take your best suit

to a dry cleaner that just opened up, whose past experience you know no nothing about. Instead, you would take less expensive garments for a while until you are certain that they know their business well, which could take years, at which time you might be ready to trust them with your more expensive items.

Emunah, therefore, refers to a belief in past successes, and it was this that God was building when He said:

> Did a people ever hear the voice of God speaking out of the midst of the fire, as you heard, and live? Has God taken a nation to Himself from the midst of another nation, through trials, signs, wonders, war, with a mighty hand, an outstretched arm, and great terrors, as God, your God, did for you in Egypt before your eyes? (Devarim 4:33-34)

Forty years later, Yehoshua—Joshua—with the help of God, conquered the nations of Canaan which the Torah states were far mightier than the Jewish people at the time. All said and done, God had proven Himself to the Jewish people in the past, that He was committed to their well-being and was prepared to turn the world upside down for their ultimate benefit.

However, it wasn't only gratitude that God wanted from the Jewish people. Rather, He wanted them to take that emunah based upon the past and project it into the future, and believe that, just as God made good on His promise of redemption in the past, He would make good on His promise of redemption in the future as well.[1] Emunah is on the past. Bitachon is on the future.

The importance of both is obvious from the perspective of the individual. The more emunah and bitachon someone has, the closer he feels to God, and usually, the holier he seems to others. More importantly, emunah and bitachon provide a sense of calm for a person caught up in a whirlpool of uncertainty, and can even result in eleventh hour solutions to overwhelming crises.

However, on a national level, emunah and bitachon are even more powerful, being an integral part of the entire redemption process:

> God said to [Moshe], "Go and gather the elders of Israel together and say to them . . ." (Shemos 3:16), because, as a result of their faith they would have merited to draw down the light of Atika Kadisha,[2] as it says in the Mechilta: "The Jewish people were redeemed from Egypt only in the merit of their faith, as it says, 'the people believed' (Shemos 4:31). Likewise, the exiles will only be gathered in the merit of their faith" (Mechilta, Beshallach 6). (Drushei Olam HaTohu, Chelek 2, Drush 5, Anaf 4 Siman 6)

---

[1] "At the time of a person's judgment after death they ask him, 'Did you anticipate the redemption?' (Shabbos 31a). What is the basis of this mitzvah? It comes from . . . 'I am God, your God, Who took you out of Egypt,' which means: Just as you must believe that I took you out [of Egypt], you must also believe that I, God your God, will gather you in and redeem you in mercy a second time." (Ohr Yechezkel, Emunas HaGeulah, 1960; p. 287)

[2] Literally, Holy Old One, a reference to a very high level of Divine, spiritual Light, with which the greatest of miracles have been performed throughout history and with which God executes redemptions for the Jewish people.

The power of emunah and bitachon to trigger redemption should not be underestimated. If the Jewish people are locked in exile, then emunah and bitachon are the keys to salvation, as they were back in Egypt:

> For their original act of faith, as it says: "the people believed and they listened" (Shemos 4:31) . . . they merited all the miracles in Egypt, and as a result of their faith and preparation of the Pesach [Offering], they merited the redemption. The flow of blessing from Above is based upon the trust that a person places in The Holy One, Blessed is He. (Drushei Olam HaTohu, Chelek 2, Drush 5, Anaf 4 Siman 6)

In other words, when the Talmud speaks about two possible times for the Final Redemption to begin, early or at the last possible moment, and two possible ways in which it can occur, respectfully or in a degrading way,[3] that is, peacefully or after the War of Gog and Magog, it is alluding to the role that emunah and bitachon play in the redemption process. They are the merit to which the Talmud refers as being necessary to bring Moshiach "hastened" and "riding on a cloud."

Hence, a lack of emunah and bitachon may not only prevent a Jew from considering moving to Eretz Yisroel in the near future, it also holds up the Final Redemption. In fact, too much self-reliance and our new-found Eisav-like pragmatism may be what has held off the Final Redemption until now. While we scratch our heads and wonder

---

[3] Sanhedrin 98a.

what is taking God so long to bring Moshiach, He may look down and wonder where all of our emunah and bitachon have gone.

Why are emunah and bitachon so important on a national level? If God saves the Jewish people, won't we believe in Him then, and in His power of salvation? Why must we make the first move and exhibit some kind of faith in Him initially, if we are to hasten the Final Redemption and bring it peacefully?

This sounds like a religious question, one that can only have a religious answer (which is probably why so many religious people take it for granted). The truth is, it is also a pragmatic question, like asking, "What must we do to avoid another world war?" It is really the same question.

Let's begin by recalling the four-fifths of the Jews that died in the Plague of Darkness in Egypt, about 12,000,000 Jews altogether. One of the reasons why it is hard to believe this happened is because one would think that such a catastrophe would be recorded somewhere in the Torah, and yet it is not, which also teaches something.

Did God simply sweep that disastrous fact under the carpet, to keep it from later generations because He knew it would put such a damper on the exodus from Egypt? After all, how does one celebrate the miraculous redemption of his nation from slavery if four-fifths of that nation didn't make it out, and were even killed by the very God that freed the remaining one-fifth?[4]

If that was the case, then the rabbis wouldn't

---

[4] Survivors of the Holocaust were grateful when it finally ended, but no one celebrated after the cruel deaths of 6,000,000 brothers and sisters.

have revealed what happened, which means that it is part of our tradition going back to Moshe Rabbeinu himself. Therefore, the exclusion of the report from the Written Law, leaving it instead for the Midrash to discuss, must be part of the lesson to be learned from their exclusion from Jewish history, indicating why emunah and bitachon are so important to the redemption process.

Every relationship, to work, requires each partner to ante up a little emunah from the beginning. If people are going to allow a relationship to develop, there has to be a certain level of faith and trust in the other side from the outset. Otherwise, the other potential partner is always suspect, or at least never taken seriously, and all efforts at building a relationship are futile.

It is emunah and bitachon that put both sides of a relationship on the same page. What we believe about life and people colors the way we perceive both, and can cause us to either read, or misread, the reality of life or the intentions of people. Misplaced trust has caused some to be taken advantage of, and the lack of it has caused others to destroy what could easily have been meaningful and productive relationships.

In Egypt, it was the difference between seeing the plagues as a path to redemption or seeing them as a way to stay in Egypt. With a little emunah and bitachon, the one-fifth that left Egypt with Moshe Rabbeinu were able to use the plagues as road signs out of Egypt. The lack of emunah and bitachon caused the four-fifths to be on a different page than God, rendering their involvement in the redemption process, and Jewish history for that matter, irrelevant.

Rabbi Yechezkel Levenstein[5] had this to say regarding this very point:

> If we examine ourselves, it seems as if we are very far from having faith in the future redemption . . . When it comes to the arrival of Moshiach and the resurrection of the dead, we are quiet, as if we are embarrassed to speak about them, as if we have given up altogether. However, the words of the Sefer Mitzvos Katan[6] should arouse trembling in our hearts since these matters are part of the mitzvah of, "I am God, your God,"[7] and anyone who is not involved with these matters is far from having any true faith . . . In truth, most of the Shemonah Esrei[8] deals with the future redemption . . . And, just as we are lacking faith in this matter, we are also distant from the essence of prayer. We lack connection to [the blessings regarding redemption], and all of our prayers are only lip service! (Ohr Yechezkel, Emunas HaGeulah, p. 287)

---

[5] Yechezkel Levenstein (1895 - 1974) was the mashgiach runchani of the Mir Yeshivah, in Mir, Belarus, and during the yeshiva's flight to Lithuania and on to Shanghai due to the invasion of Poland by Nazi Germany in World War II. He was a leader of several yeshivos in Europe, America, and Israel after the war, including the Mir in Jerusalem and Ponevezh in Bnai Brak.

[6] Literally, the Small Book of Mitzvos, also known by its acronym, SeMaK. It was written by Rabbi Yitzchak ben Yosef of Corbeil, France (c. 1210-1280), and it was a codification of the commandments, and included contemporary halachic issues, as well as midrash and ethics.

[7] The first of the Ten Commandments, and a fundamental of fundamentals of Jewish belief.

[8] The main part of the daily prayer service, the Shemonah Esrai, also called the Amidah, is comprised of 19 blessings.

One of the ironies of learning Torah is that it can be done without really being on the same page as God. People can do mitzvos all day long and still be oblivious to what God values most. Both can earn a Jew reward in the World-to-Come, but neither necessarily guarantees a Jew a ticket to redemption, as history has testified countless times before.

To be invited to redemption, a Jew has to be on the same page as God, the same redemption page as God. He has to believe in it, anticipate it, want it daily, and be pained by the fact that it has yet to arrive. His life has to revolve around the idea that the Final Redemption could come at any moment, and the need to be ready physically and spiritually for it.

From that perspective, all of a sudden, living in Israel becomes a lot more appealing, and a great way to express one's emunah and bitachon in God and His promise of redemption.

ten
the big picture

ONE OF THE most fascinating—and frightening—features about people is how so many can look at the same thing and see something different. As a result, one person's good is another person's evil, one person's hero is another's enemy.

To be human is to be subjective. It is to put a personal spin on the events of life, so that they fit in with one's own personal idea of what life should be like. Everyone likes to be comfortable and secure, and people would rather distort the general reality to suit their own than to change theirs to suit the general reality.

The problem with this approach is obvious, though often taken for granted. We think that we can outsmart the general reality, when instead, it simply tolerates our subjective points of view until it can no longer. When that happens, a boom is usually lowered, resulting in some kind of rude awakening for mankind. The Holocaust was the most recent.

There is an Objective Reality. This was the point that God made when He gave the Torah to the Jewish people over three millennia ago. A certain amount of subjectivity is not only natural, it is healthy, important for creativity, and even enjoyed by God—but only until it runs contrary to His Objective Reality.

The Objective Reality is the Big Picture of history. Unlike our human, subjective realities, the Big Picture takes into account everything, in a way that only God can. It includes the entire past, and everything destined to occur in the future, and all of it is embedded in the Torah from the Bais[1] of "Bereishis" until the Lamed[2] of "Yisroel."

This Big Picture is also multi-layered, comprising what the Midrash calls the 70 Facets of Torah,[3] and Kabbalah calls Pardes, which means orchard, but which is a reference to the four levels on which Torah can be learned.[4] By moving from one intellectual level to the next, one gains greater access to God's Objective Reality, which provides a mind's-eye vision of Creation and history far greater than any human eye can behold:

---

[1] The second letter of the Aleph-Bais, and the first letter of first word, Bereishis—in the beginning—in the Torah.

[2] The 12th letter of the Aleph-Bais, and the the last letter of the last word of the entire Torah.

[3] There are 70 facets to Torah. (Zohar, Bereishis 36)

[4] Although Pardes is a Hebrew word, in this case it is an acronym for: Pshat—Simple Understanding, Remez—Hint, Drush—Exegesis, and Sod —Secret (Sha'ar HaGilgulim, Ch. 11).

With the light[5] that The Holy One, Blessed is He, created on the first day, Adam looked and was able to see from one end of the world until the other. (Chagigah 12a)

Obviously, we are not talking about a physical light here, since physical light could never provide such a view.[6] Rather, the Talmud has to be talking about an intellectual light, one that is seen not with our physical eyes, but with our mind's eye, one which provides a person with a comprehensive understanding and appreciation of all of history.

This may all sound somewhat esoteric, and perhaps, even somewhat irrelevant. Until, that is, it helps to answer the question:

Why do the Jewish people tend to suffer terribly at the end of every exile, and lose all or most of their hard-earned possessions?

If a person believes that God runs the world, and accepts the Talmud's assertion that everything that occurs is a result of Divine Providence,[7] then whatever has happened to Jews throughout history has also been the result of His Providence, the good and the bad.

According to such a world view, there are two possible answers to the question above: Either God doesn't warn us about the danger He is bringing

---

[5] This is the light of Torah, as it says: Torah is the blueprint for Creation (Bereishis Rabbah 1:1). These concepts are dealt with extensively in my books, The Big Picture, Redemption to Redemption, The Light of 36, and The Equation of Life.

[6] This idea is dealt with extensively in my book, The Light of Thirty-Six.

[7] Chullin 7b. This is accepted fact in Kabbalah.

our way, or He warns us, but we don't take His warnings seriously. Even though it says:

> I will be gracious to whom I will be gracious, and I will show mercy to whom I will show mercy. (Shemos 33:19)

the second reason is the most likely:

> God told Moshe, "I have seen this people, and they are stiff-necked." (Shemos 32:9)[8]

However, not all stubbornness is born of simple obstinance. Sometimes it is the result of faulty assumptions and perspectives, or too much subjective reality and not enough Big Picture reality. European Jewry would have been less stubborn about leaving Europe in the 1930s if they had known in advance what was coming and why; if they had known that Nazi Germany was destined to bring the European part of the final exile to an abrupt end.

How could they have possibly known such an important fact, any more than Spanish Jewry could have known that the Inquisition and subsequent exile from Spain would do the same at their time in history? The answer in two words: Big Picture.

This is because there is another name for the Big Picture: the Master Plan, something that, un-

---

[8] God's concern for the well-being of the Jewish people is expressed in many places, including here: "If you will diligently listen to the voice of God, your God, and do what is right in His eyes, listen to His commandments and keep all His statutes, I will not inflict you with any of the diseases which I inflicted Egypt with, for I am God who heals you" (Shemos 15:26).

fortunately, tends to become of extreme importance only once Jewish suffering goes beyond
normal comprehension. It is what caused many
"mainstream" Jews to turn to the Zohar during
the Middle Ages, and the writings of the Arizal in
the 17th century, as they tried to make some
sense of the situation that was torturing them to
death.[9]

All of a sudden, when the situation of the
Jewish people defies subjective logic, subjective
reality becomes ineffective, by a long shot, to guide
us from day-to-day. We are forced, by unreason-
able crises, to seek out a bigger picture which we
believe, in the back of our minds, has to exist as
much God Himself has to exist.

This was not always the case. In ancient
times, for example, when it came to the idea of the
Divine, worshippers believed it was possible for a
god to act out powerfully, and sometimes even
cruelly, against all logic. All a person could do was
hope it never happened to him, and that if it did,
the results wouldn't be fatal.

Judaism, however, revealed that not only is
there one God, but that He made Creation, runs
history, and acts logically, even if His logic sometimes eludes man. Unlike the ancient gods, the
Jewish God does not suffer from any lack, and certainly does not suffer from any human failings.
Whatever God does He always does with purpose,
with ultimate purpose. This is a fundamental of
Torah belief.

Even more amazing, God, on many occasions,
has shared His plans with man, even giving us the

---

[9] Triumph of Survival: The Story of the Jews in the Modern Era
1650-1990, Wein, Berel, 1990, p. 3.

Torah to keep track of them. He even gave us prophets to help us stay in touch with the Master Plan of Creation, so that we can help fulfill it and be rewarded for doing so. And, when all else fails, He uses Hashgochah Pratis—Divine Providence—to steer us once we lose the ability to steer ourselves.

The problem, historically, arises when we insist on sticking to our subjective realities at a time that they run contrary to the Objective Reality, which has become insistent. It does that when history reaches a keitz, literally, an end point, a moment in time and within a period in history during which something significant has to happen for the sake of some redemption.[10]

If the Jewish people realize this, and get with the program, the transition from one period of history to the next is smooth. If we do not realize it, and even obstruct the path of transition, then, well, in the past we have often been steamrolled by it. The objectives of a keitz are always achieved, either because of the Jewish people or through them.

This is why Ya'akov Avinu, on his deathbed, tried, unsuccessfully, to reveal the final keitz to his sons:[11] He wanted to make sure that, when it finally came around, we'd be able to recognize it, and work with it and not against it. However, apparently God had other plans.[12]

Where does that leave all subsequent generations, if Ya'akov Avinu himself could not receive

---

[10] Sanhedrin 97b.
[11] Bereishis 49:1.
[12] Apparently, the brothers had not become unified enough to receive this prophecy. See my book, The Light of ThirtySix for the full story.

foreknowledge of the Final Redemption? Are we simply destined to suffer through it, which is why he was denied the prophecy in the first place?

Not necessarily. Though some things in Jewish history have become less clear with time, or forgotten altogether, some things have become more revealed. Even modern technology has played a role in helping us better understand some of the more abstract Torah concepts, providing everyday physical examples of what once were difficult abstract ideas.[13]

The Zohar itself wasn't even published until the 13th century,[14] and the Arizal, who helped us to better understand it, didn't live until the 1500s. Even the printing press, which allowed for a more accurate and better quality reproduction, as well as a wider distribution of the written word, wasn't invented until 1440 CE.

Hence, it says:

> When Yemos HaMoshiach approaches, knowledge will increase in the world, and even children will find and know wisdom of the secrets; they will know keitzin and calculations for redemption . . . (Zohar, Vayaira 118a)

In the end, however, it is not really a question of being able to calculate the precise moment of Moshiach's arrival. It is about paying attention to the world around us, and where we are holding as a nation historically. It is about entertaining the

---

[13] For example, a modern day electrical grid can help one understand the system of the Sefiros, the basis of all of Creation on a Kabbalistic level.

[14] 1240 CE.

possibility that our perspectives on Jewish history, and its events, are not as complete as we'd like to believe they are.

Then, it is about finding out what we are missing and updating our perspectives until our subjective realities more closely match God's Objective Reality. Learning Torah and doing mitzvos are essential, but they are not always enough when it comes to being on the same page of history as God.

This is what tells a Jew what God is thinking, and why. This is what tells him where to live, and when. It is what allows him to figure out on his own where he is safest, and where and how to invest his money. It teaches him that safety for a Jew is defined as being where God wants you to be, when God wants you to be there.

For example, a Jew can be right next to a major conflict, but if that is where God wants him to be, then he will be safe, even if it takes a miracle to guarantee it. Or, he can be 6,000 miles away from a danger-zone, but if it is not where God wants him to be, then he can be at greater risk than in the actual place of danger.[15]

Not only this, but being on the same page as God, when it comes to the unfolding of history, opens a person up to even greater Hashgochah Pratis. We may not merit prophecy, but we can merit other forms of Divine assistance that can help us to see what we must see, and hear what we

---

[15] More Jews died in the attack on the Twin Towers in downtown New York on September 11, 2001, than did in the attack on the Sbarro restaurant in downtown Jerusalem a month before. Obviously, those who died in New York, which included five Israelis, were not necessarily in New York to avoid living in Israel. However, it does make the point that a Jew can be in even greater danger far away from what the world calls a "Danger Zone."

must hear, at the most opportune time to do so.

This book has tried to provide a bit of a glimpse at the Big Picture, in an attempt to guide people to survival at the End-of-Days, as unrealistic as that sounds. But if it is as close as many think it is, it wouldn't be the first time that the Jewish people have been caught completely off guard by an event of Biblical proportions.

eleven
a final word

WHEN I USED to ask people why they had no desire to make aliyah, most answered: Parnassah—Finances. There was nothing spectacular about that answer, as it has been the same one given for decades now.

After all, in Israel, a country that has a population that is a fraction of a fraction of the population of other more developed countries, such as the United States and England, and few natural resources other than sun, wind, and intelligence, how can one make a decent living? These people either had good jobs already, or were certain to find one; jobs that they assumed did not exist for them in Eretz Yisroel.

One day something strange occurred to me:

Why isn't anyone concerned, first and foremost, about the fact that tiny little Eretz Yisroel is surrounded by hundreds of millions of enemies who probably do little else all day other than plan the complete and utter destruction of the "Zionist State." Why doesn't anyone ever mention that as a reason not to make aliyah?

Even funnier, I thought, was how many of these people not only travel to Eretz Yisroel—straight into the Lion's Den—they even allow their children to attend yeshivah or seminary there. This meant one of two things: Either they did not like their children, or, though the parnassah issue loomed large, for them the defense issue loomed small.

It's not so hard to understand why: Israel is still here.

Unquestionably, the survival of the modern state has been miraculous the entire way through. This is especially evident from the fact that, as mentioned earlier, Israelis have not only survived, they have thrived, both materially and spiritually. This has earned them, and more importantly, God, the admiration of many gentiles, and the adulation of many Diaspora Jews.

Not so, though, when it comes to the parnassah of individual Israelis. The Jewish State has been on the receiving end of charity for as long as it has existed, and many people who have made aliyah have returned to the Diaspora because of financial difficulties. For some reason, many seem to assume, God has not been able to keep up His financial end of the bargain as well as He has the defense end.

If that is true, however, then it is deliberate, because obviously God can do whatever He wants, whenever He wants, in whatever manner He chooses. Indeed, as the Torah makes clear, there is a reason why making a living is the test of every Jew:

> God told Moshe, "I have heard the Jewish people's complaints. Tell them, in the evening they will eat meat, and in the morning they will be satiated with bread, and you will know that I am God, your God." (Shemos 16:11-12)

These verses, of course, are talking about the mann, the miraculous bread that rained down upon the Jewish people their entire 40-year journey in the desert. Nothing represents parnassah better than bread itself, the staple of life, and apparently, nothing makes it clear that God is our God more than parnassah.

We first learn this from Avraham Avinu:

> Avram said to the king of Sodom, "I have vowed to God, the Most High, the Owner of Heaven and Earth! I will not take even a thread to a shoelace from anything of yours. You will not say, 'I made Avram rich'." (Bereishis 14:22-23)

Even though Avraham had earned his spoils of war by defeating the enemy kings, he rejected them out of concern that others would not see his parnassah as having come directly from God. He wanted it to be perfectly clear that the same God Who had promised him wealth[1] was the same God

---

[1] Bereishis 12:2.

Who had delivered it.[2]

An even clearer example is Ya'akov Avinu's response to his dream of the ladder reaching up into Heaven:

> Ya'akov made a vow saying, "If God will be with me, and take care of me on the path I am going, and give me bread to eat and clothes to wear, and then bring me back in peace to my father's house, then God will be my God." (Bereishis 28:20-21)

Isn't God our God everywhere, no matter what He does for us? Did anyone know this better than Ya'akov Avinu? Then what did he mean? He meant what was implied by the blessing he received from his father just prior to going on his journey:

> "May God give you of the dew of Heaven, and the fat of the land with much grain and wine." (Bereishis 27:28)

When Yitzchak gave this blessing to Ya'akov, he wasn't just blessing him with good parnassah, as evident from the blessing he later gave to Eisav for good parnassah as well. The difference between the two blessings, as Rashi points out, was the inclusion of the Name of God in Ya'akov's blessing, and its obvious exclusion from Eisav's blessing.

In other words, Yitzchak told Ya'akov: "It is

---

[2] Hence, he had no problem accepting wealth from Pharaoh, who gave it to Avraham only because of the obvious miracle God had performed to save Sarah from being taken by Pharaoh (Bereishis 12:20).

one thing to receive parnassah, but something altogether different to receive parnassah in a manner that makes it completely clear that it is from God. My blessing is that you should merit an income that makes it clear that everything you receive is from God."

This is the goal. Making an income is not only about material survival, but about spiritual survival as well, which means always being intellectually and emotionally clear about its Source. This is why in Birchas HaMazon,[3] one of the several times a week we thank God for our parnassah, we make the following request:

> May it be that we never need, God, our God, either gifts from people or their loans, except from Your full, open, holy, and generous Hand.

If we refuse to receive gifts or take loans from people, how do we plan to receive them from God? Rather, we ask God that if and when we receive parnassah through others, that it should be in a way that we never lose sight of the fact that they are merely conduits for His love and generosity.[4]

Having said that, it is noteworthy how the Torah closes out the section discussing the new blessing of mann:

---

[3] Usually translated as Grace After Meals.

[4] The average fundraiser knows what this means, because there are donors who make you feel as if you are taking food from their children when they give, and therefore, expect eternal gratitude, others who reject praise, claiming instead that they are merely a conduit for God's generosity, and many in-between these two extremes. On occasion, I have even been thanked for giving them the opportunity to give to a Torah cause.

The Jewish people ate mann for 40 years, until they came to inhabited land. They ate mann until they came to the border of Canaan. (Shemos 16:35)

In other words, the mann ceased to fall as the Jewish people were about to cross the border into Eretz Yisroel. However, if the main point of the mann was food, then it should have lasted even into Eretz Yisroel, since it could take time to find food for everyone, especially with war on the agenda.

But, if the point of the mann was to make it perfectly clear that God is our God, then the Talmud has already said:

All those who dwell in Eretz Yisroel are like those with a God, and all those who dwell outside the Land are like those without a God. (Kesuvos 110b)

"For they have driven me out this day that I should not cleave to the inheritance of God, saying: 'Go, serve other gods' " (I Shmuel 26:19). Did someone tell Dovid, "Serve other gods"? Rather, [this is intended] to tell you that whoever lives outside the Land may be regarded as one who worships idols. (Kesuvos 110b)

Thus, whatever the mann was for the Jewish people in the desert for 40 years, in terms of closing the gap between making a living and closeness to God, Eretz Yisroel is for the Jew—forever. This was the point that the prophet Yirmiyahu made to the Jews in his time, as Rashi explains:

Moshe told Aharon, "Take one jar and put a full omer[5] of mann into it; place it before God for a safekeeping for your generations." (Shemos 16:33)

In the days of Yirmiyahu, when he would rebuke [the Jewish people], saying, "Why do you not engage in Torah [study]? and they would answer, "If we stop working and engage in Torah, how will we earn a living?" He would bring out before them the jar of mann and say to them, "You! See the word of God!" It does not say "hear," but "see," [indicating that he showed them the jar of mann for them to see. He would tell them,] "With this [mann] your ancestors sustained themselves; God has many messengers to prepare nourishment for those who fear Him." (Rashi)

They didn't have or need mann in Eretz Yisroel, only the lesson it taught. It was to tell them, us, that by trusting in God in any generation for our parnassah, we leave room for Him to take care of us supernaturally. It's part of the deal we have with God when we live on His Land.

When we live on His Land.

---

[5] Equal in amount to 2.2 quarts.

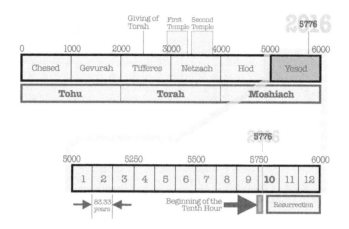

The Tenth Hour of History

1. The top bar shows how the six sefiros correspond to the six millennia of history. Each sefirah is the basis of all that occurred during its corresponding millennium.

2. The second bar shows how the 6000 years are divided into three periods of history: "Tohu," or Creation until 2000, "Torah," from Avraham's 52nd year until 4000, and "Moshiach," from 4000 until 6000 (Sanhedrin 97a).

3. The third bar expands the sixth millennium and divides it into 12 periods of 83.33 years each (Sanhedrin 38b), showing the "Tenth Hour" of history.

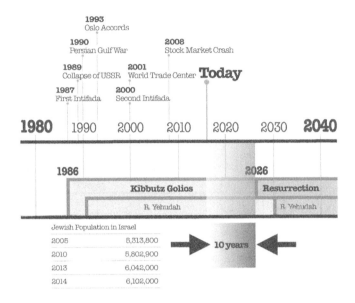

Recent Events

1. The top area shows significant historical events that have occurred over the last 30 years.

2. The second bar is the timeline from 1980–2040.

3. The two bars inside the timeline are the two opinions in the Zohar regarding the official beginning of Kibbutz Golios, the ingathering of Jewish exiles from around the world. It also shows the beginning of the period called the "Resurrection of the Dead."

4. The numbers below this show the waves of yah.

Aliyah means ascension, and refers to moving to Israel from other lands, which are considered to be on a lower level, spiritually-speaking.

Atika Kadisha is Aramaic for Holy Old One, the name of one of the highest level in the sefiros, spiritual transformers, so-to-speak, through which God filters His Divine light to maintain Creation. As such, it is the level of light with which God performs great miracles and carries out Jewish redemptions.

Bitachon means trust, but usually refers specifically to trust in God. See Chapter Eight for a more comprehensive definition.

Chevlei Moshiach refers to the "birth pangs" of Moshiach, because just as childbirth is a painful process with a positive end, likewise is the "birth" of Moshiach into history one in which darkness precedes the dawn.

Chillul Hashem means profanation of the Name, and refers to any act, speech, or thought that reduces the reality of God in Creation, the exact opposite of Kiddush Hashem (see below). The word chillul comes from the word challal, which means a void, which is what a Chillul Hashem creates: a void of Divine light.

Chofetz Chaim was Rabbi Yisroel Meir (Kagan) Poupko (1838-1933), nicknamed after one of his most famous works of the same name written to spiritually refine the behavior of his fellow Jews. As well as being known for his extreme piety, he was a leading Talmudist, Halachist, and Ethicist whose works and words remain extremely influential even today.

Chutz L'Aretz literally means outside the Land, referring to any land beyond the borders of Israel.

Eisav was Esau, Jacob's twin brother.

Elokim is one of the Biblical Names of God, which tradition teaches refers to God as the Source of all existence and forces in Creation. It is pronounced Elokim in deference to God, but it is actually spelled with a Heh, not a Kuf, which when transliterated, would have an "h" replace the "k."

Emunah means faith. See Chapter Eight for a more comprehensive definition.

Eretz Yisroel is the Land of Israel.

Gehinom is the purgatory that unrectified sinners have to endure in preparation for the World-to-Come.

Gog, according to the Septuagint, is from the word Agag, a generic name used for kings of Amalek, the nemesis and anti-thesis of the Jewish people. Tradition teaches that Gog, whichever nation they will be at the End of Days, will join with Magog (see below), whichever nation they will be at that time, in the last war of history, against the Jewish people, meant to be threshold to the Messianic Era.

Halachah, which refers to Torah law, is derived from the word that means walk, since Torah law is the path a Jew is meant to walk in life.

Hashem literally means "the name," but it used to refer to The Name, God's Four-Letter name that we do not pronounce as it is written because of its level of holiness. Therefore, as a matter of respect, it is commonly used to refer to God Himself.

Hashkofah literally means outlook, and therefore, it refers to one's philosophy about life.

Hashgochah Pratis literally means personal providence, but it refers to Divine Providence, particularly on the level that it operates in Israel, that is, in a more personal and overt manner. Hashgochah Klallis, or General Providence, as the name implies, refers to a more covert level of Divine involvement in the affairs of man, and the level of Divine Providence in the Diaspora

Kabbalah refers to that which has been received, which in this case was a tradition of Torah study on an esoteric level. It is also referred to as Sod, which means secret, because Kabbalah contains many hidden insights about Torah and Creation in general.

Keitz means end, or extreme, and therefore is also used to refer to times of redemption, which are always turning points in history. The Final Redemption, therefore, is called Keitz HaYomim—the End-of-Days.

Kibbutz Golios is the ingathering—kibbutz—of Jewish exiles—golios—from around the world to Israel, which the Torah states will occur as part of the Final Redemption.

Kiddush Hashem means sanctification of the Name, and refers to any act, speech, or thought that increases the reality of God in Creation. It does not necessarily mean that others will acknowledge this positive change in Creation; they may, in fact, even mock it. The important thing is that an act, speech, or thought has drawn more Divine light into the world.

Leshem Shevo v'Achlamah was Rabbi Shlomo

Elyashiv (1841-1928), who was considered to be one of the greatest Kabbalists and righteous people of his time. He wrote many works, all of which deal with the process of Creation, as Kabbalah understands it, up to the point where the Torah begins with the start of physical Creation. One such work, quoted extensively here, is Drushei Olam HaTohu, literally, Exegesis of the World of Void, because as the second verse of the Torah states, Tohu, or Void (also translated as chaos), was part of the Creation process. However, he also provided Kabbalah's understanding of history, and of events to come, such as the Messianic Era, the Resurrection of the Dead, and the World-to-Come.

Magog is first mentioned in the Torah as one of the 70 nations that descended from Noach; in this case, from his son Yefes (Bereishis 10:2). Targum Yonason identifies Magog with Germania (I Divrei HaYamim 1:5), but the Talmud Yerushalmi (Megillah 1:9) says they became the Goths, who migrated to Scythia in what is now southern Russia. Others say that the Mongols may have been from Magog.

Mann is a Hebrew transliteration of what is usually translated as manna, the miraculous bread that descended from the sky each day for the Jewish people over the 40 years in they traveled the desert.

Midrash is a part of the Oral Law section of the Torah that provides background information, often, but not necessarily, in story form. Some midrashim are on the Torah itself, and opinions vary as to whether each one is to be taken literally. Some are on later works, such as the Talmud, and clearly are not all literal. Regardless, in each case, the message is a principle of Torah.

Mitzvos are Torah commandments.

Pardes means orchard, but in Kabbalah it is an acronym for the words Pshat, Remez, Drush, and Sod—Simple, Hint, Exegesis, and Secret—which are four different levels of Torah learning. They also corresponds to four different areas of Torah learning: Torah verse, Mishnah, Talmud, and Kabbalah, respectively.

Parnassah is the term for financial support, usually with respect to earning a living.

Rabbeinu means our rabbi, used mostly, but not exclusively, in reference to a rabbi and leader of great Torah stature, such as in, Moshe Rabbeinu—our rabbi, leader, teacher, etc.

Rashi is an acronym for Rabbi Shlomo Yitzchaki (1040-1104), who is the foremost commentator on Tanach and the Talmud. Though others may argue with him, his word is extremely authoritative.

Shechinah is the Name for the Divine Presence, from the word shochen, which means dwell, since the Shechinah dwells within Creation.

Shechinah b'Golus means that when the Jewish people go into golus—exile—the Divine Presence accompanies them. Even though God is everywhere in the world at all times, He allows His Presence to be more obvious in Israel, and to the Jewish people in the Diaspora, somewhat, when they are there for Divinely-sanctioned for reasons.

Shemonah Esrai means eighteen, a reference to the original eighteen blessings that are the main section of weekday prayer service. It is also called Amidah, which means standing, because the Shemonah Esrai is supposed to be said while standing out of respect for God. Eventually, an additional blessing was added in the time of the Roman occupation because of the increase of informers against the Jewish people. However, the name remained even after the number of blessings became nineteen.

Tanach is the way the Hebrew acronym Tav-Nun-Chof is pronounced, and refers to Torah, Nevi'im, and Kesuvim, or the Torah, the Book of Prophets, and the Writings.

Techiyas HaMeisim means resurrection of the dead, a period in the future when the dead will be recreated anew from the ground like the first man, free of all spiritual impurities in preparation for eternal life in the World-to-Come that follows. Many believe that this period takes place after Year 6000, but according to the Leshem, based upon the Zohar (Midrash Ne'elam), it occurs in advance of 6000.

Tehillim is Hebrew for Psalms.

Teshuvah means return, and is the word for repentance.

Torah principally refers to the Five Books of Moses, but it can also be used as a general term of reference for all Torah concepts.

Tzedakah is the Torah term for charity. It is derived from the word that means righteousness because, unlike charity, which a person may give merely because it feels good to do so, tzedakah is performed first and foremost because God has commanded us to give it. This intention elevates to charity to the level of righteousness.

Vilna Gaon means Genius of Vilna, and it refers to Rabbi Eliyahu ben Shlomo Zalman Kremer (1720-1797), who was an acknowledged leading Talmudist, Halachist, and Kabbalist, and the foremost leader of Ashkenazic Jewry over the past few centuries. He is also called the GR"A, whose letters stand for Gaon Rabbeinu Eliyahu.

Ya'akov Avinu, or Jacob our Father, was the third of the three Forefathers.

Yemos HaMoshiach is literally the Days of Moshiach, which is the Messianic Era.

Fundamentals of Reincarnation

15-Session Course Based Upon Sha'ar HaGilgulim

Though the original Hebrew version of Sha'ar HaGilgulim is less than 200 pages, the translated and annotated version is much longer and far more de-tailed. To make some of the material, especially sections relevant to everyday life, more readily accessible, fundamentals of reincarnation have organized into a 15-session course that is available online through Juniversity or Udemy. The course is an amazing overview of many life-altering concepts, and topics include:

- What is "Pardes"?
- What Are The Sefiros?
- The Five Levels of Soul
- What Is An Adam Shalaim?
- What is Reincarnation?
- Reasons To Reincarnate
- Leaving The Realm of Impurity

- Famous Reincarnations
- Reincarnations of Moshe Rabbeinu
- The Ten Martyrs
- Reincarnation & Resurrection
- Achieving Personal Perfection
- Return of the Generation of the Desert
- Moshiach & Redemption

The course includes PDF, Mp3, and video presentations, all of which are available through Juniversity or Udemy.

If self-knowledge, fulfillment, and personal rectification talks to you, then so will this course.

Enroll now.

Sha'ar HaGilgulim

Many cultures discuss the concept of reincarnation, but how many have an authoritative work on the topic? How many provide as much detail into the concept of personal rectification as "Sha'ar HaGilgulim," or "Gate of Reincarnations"? And how many of those works have been translated into English, annotated, and made available in hardcover, pdf, and kindle formats?

Hardcover and PDF formats available through the OnLine Bookstore at Thirtysix.org. Kindle format available through Amazon Kindle.

essays, books,
video, audio that
which change
the way you look
at life and
history

Made in United States
North Haven, CT
20 October 2021